WORLD ATLAS

Maps supplied by DK Cartography.

A Funfax Book
Copyright © 1998 Funfax Ltd,
Woodbridge, Suffolk, IP12 1AN, England.
All rights reserved.

CONTENTS

KEY

POPULATED PLACES

◉ Capital city
  greater than 500,000

◎ Capital city
  100,000 - 500,000

• Capital city
  Less than 100,000

◉ Greater than 500,000

◉ 100,000 - 500,000

○ Less than 100,000

—— International
  border

〜 State border

〜〜 River

〜〜 Seasonal river

Lake

Seasonal lake

—— Road

—— Railway

······ Summer pack ice
  limit

Winter pack ice
  limit

✈ International
  airport

△ Spot height
  - metres

THE PHYSICAL WORLD

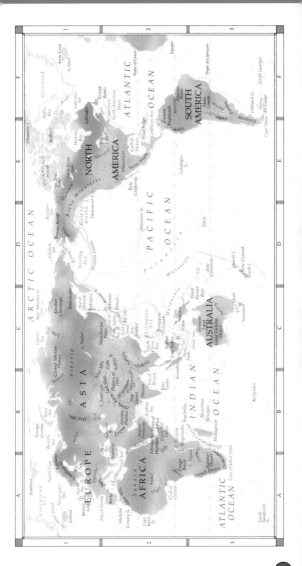

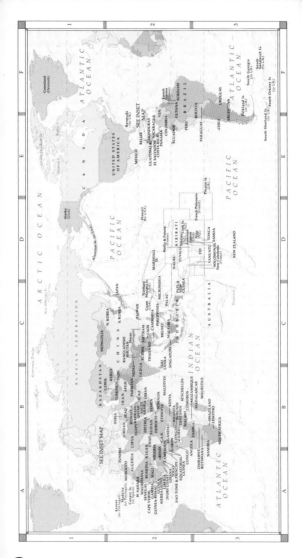

POLITICAL EUROPE

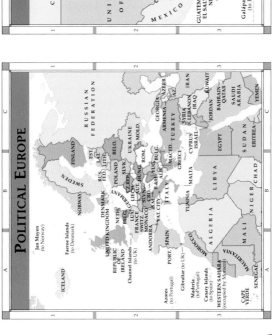

Jan Mayen (to Norway)

Faeroe Islands (to Denmark)

ICELAND

REPUBLIC OF IRELAND

UNITED KINGDOM

Channel Islands (to UK)

NORWAY

SWEDEN

FINLAND

EST

LAT

LITH

RUS. FED.

DENMARK

NETH.

BELG.

LUX.

GERMANY

POLAND

BELO.

UKRAINE

RUSSIAN FEDERATION

CZECH

SLVK.

MOLD.

AUST. HUNG.

ROM.

FRANCE

SWITZ.

SLOVEN.

CRO.

B.&H.

YUG.

BULG.

ANDORRA

MONACO

VAT. CITY

ITALY

MACED.

GEORGIA

ARMENIA

AZERB.

ALB.

GREECE

TURKEY

IRAN

PORT.

SPAIN

SARD.

SICILY

MALTA

TUNISIA

CYPRUS

ISRAEL

SYRIA

LEBANON

IRAQ

KUWAIT

Gibraltar (to UK)

MOROCCO

ALGERIA

LIBYA

EGYPT

JORDAN

BAHRAIN

QATAR

SAUDI ARABIA

Madeira (to Portugal)

Azores (to Portugal)

Canary Islands (to Spain)

WESTERN SAHARA (occupied by Morocco)

MAURITANIA

MALI

NIGER

CHAD

SUDAN

ERITREA

YEMEN

SENEGAL

CAPE VERDE

POLITICAL CARIBBEAN

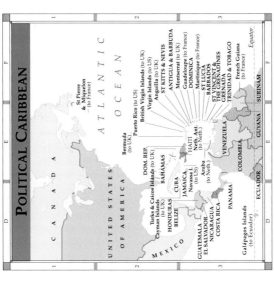

A T L A N T I C   O C E A N

C A N A D A

UNITED STATES OF AMERICA

MEXICO

Bermuda (to UK)

St Pierre & Miquelon (to France)

Puerto Rico (to US)

British Virgin Islands (to UK)

Virgin Islands (to US)

Anguilla (to UK)

ST KITTS & NEVIS

ANTIGUA & BARBUDA

Montserrat (to UK)

Guadeloupe (to France)

Martinique (to France)

DOMINICA

ST LUCIA

BARBADOS

ST VINCENT & THE GRENADINES

GRENADA

TRINIDAD & TOBAGO

French Guiana (to France)

DOM. REP.

HAITI

Navassa I. (to US)

Neth. Ant. (to Neth)

BAHAMAS

Turks & Caicos Islands (to UK)

CUBA

JAMAICA

Aruba (to Neth)

Cayman Islands (to UK)

BELIZE

HONDURAS

GUATEMALA

EL SALVADOR

NICARAGUA

COSTA RICA

PANAMA

VENEZUELA

COLOMBIA

GUYANA

SURINAM

ECUADOR

Galápagos Islands (to Ecuador)

Equator

5

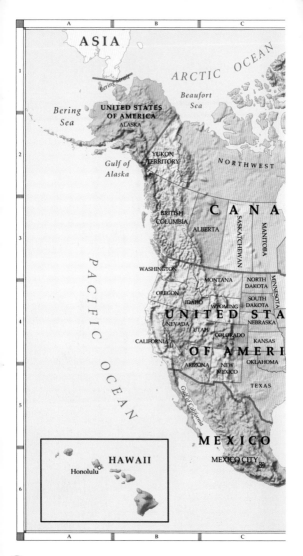

ASIA

ARCTIC OCEAN

Bering Strait

Beaufort Sea

Bering Sea

UNITED STATES OF AMERICA
ALASKA

YUKON TERRITORY

Gulf of Alaska

NORTHWEST

CANA

BRITISH COLUMBIA

ALBERTA

SASKATCHEWAN

MANITOBA

PACIFIC OCEAN

WASHINGTON

MONTANA

NORTH DAKOTA

MINNESOTA

OREGON

IDAHO

WYOMING

SOUTH DAKOTA

UNITED STA

NEVADA

UTAH

NEBRASKA

COLORADO

OF AMERI

CALIFORNIA

KANSAS

ARIZONA

NEW MEXICO

OKLAHOMA

TEXAS

Gulf of California

MEXICO

MEXICO CITY

HAWAII

Honolulu

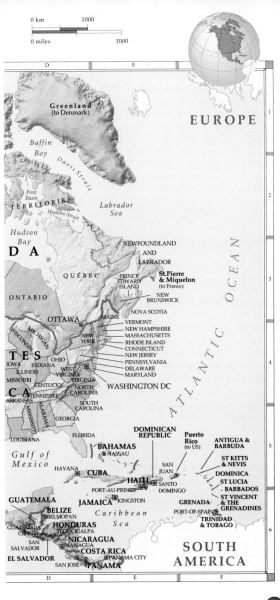

Map labels

Scale
0 km   1000
0 miles   1000

Greenland
(to Denmark)

EUROPE

Baffin
Bay

Davis Strait

Foxe
Basin

TERRITORIES

Labrador
Sea

Hudson Strait

Hudson
Bay

D A

NEWFOUNDLAND
AND
LABRADOR

QUÉBEC

PRINCE
EDWARD
ISLAND

St.Pierre
& Miquelon
(to France)

ONTARIO

NEW
BRUNSWICK

NOVA SCOTIA

OTTAWA

MAINE

VERMONT

WISCONSIN

MICHIGAN

NEW HAMPSHIRE

MASSACHUSETTS

RHODE ISLAND

CONNECTICUT

NEW
YORK

OHIO

NEW JERSEY

IOWA

INDIANA

PENNSYLVANIA

ILLINOIS

WEST
VIRGINIA

DELAWARE

MARYLAND

TES

MISSOURI

KENTUCKY

VIRGINIA

WASHINGTON DC

CA

ARKANSAS

TENNESSEE

NORTH
CAROLINA

MISSISSIPPI

ALABAMA

SOUTH
CAROLINA

GEORGIA

ATLANTIC OCEAN

LOUISIANA

FLORIDA

DOMINICAN
REPUBLIC

Puerto
Rico
(to US)

ANTIGUA &
BARBUDA

Gulf of
Mexico

BAHAMAS

NASSAU

ST KITTS
& NEVIS

HAVANA

CUBA

SAN
JUAN

DOMINICA

HAITI

ST LUCIA

BARBADOS

PORT-AU-PRINCE

SANTO
DOMINGO

GUATEMALA

JAMAICA

Kingston

ST VINCENT
& THE
GRENADINES

BELIZE

BELMOPAN

Caribbean

GRENADA

PORT-OF-SPAIN

GUATEMALA
CITY

HONDURAS

Sea

TRINIDAD
& TOBAGO

SAN
SALVADOR

TEGUCIGALPA

NICARAGUA

EL SALVADOR

MANAGUA

COSTA RICA

SOUTH
AMERICA

SAN JOSÉ

PANAMA

PANAMA CITY

7

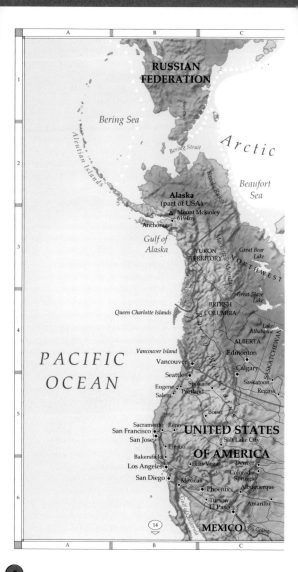

RUSSIAN FEDERATION

Bering Sea

Arctic

Bering Strait

Aleutian Islands

Alaska
(part of USA)
△ Mount Mckinley
6194m

Anchorage

Gulf of Alaska

Brooks Range

Beaufort Sea

YUKON TERRITORY

Mackenzie Mountains

Great Bear Lake

NORTHWEST

Great Slave Lake

BRITISH COLUMBIA

Queen Charlotte Islands

Lake Athabasca

ALBERTA

SASKATCHEWAN

Rocky Mountains

Vancouver Island

Edmonton

Vancouver

Calgary

Seattle

Spokane

Saskatoon

PACIFIC OCEAN

Eugene · Portland
Salem

Regina

Boise

Sacramento · Reno

UNITED STATES

San Francisco

Salt Lake City

San Jose

· Fresno

OF AMERICA

Bakersfield

Las Vegas

Denver

Los Angeles

Colorado

Colorado Springs

San Diego

Mexicali

· Phoenix

Albuquerque

Tucson

Amarillo

El Paso

Gulf of California

MEXICO

Rio Grande

0 km 600

0 miles 600

SWEDEN
NORWAY
Svalbard
(to Norway)

Norwegian Sea

Ocean

ICELAND

Ellesmere
Island

Greenland
(to Denmark)

REYKJAVÍK

Arctic Circle

Baffin Bay

Victoria
Island

Baffin Island

Davis Strait

TERRITORIES

Foxe
Basin

*Labrador
Sea*

Hudson Strait

Reindeer
Lake

Hudson
Bay

NEWFOUNDLAND
AND LABRADOR

C A N A D A

MANITOBA

QUÉBEC

St John's
Newfoundland

Lake
Winnipeg

ONTARIO

St-Pierre and
Miquelon
(to France)

Winnipeg

Thunder Bay

Québec
Montreal

Halifax

Minneapolis

Lake
Superior

OTTAWA

Sioux
Falls

Lake
Michigan

Lake
Huron

Lake
Ontario

Albany
Boston

Hartford

Omaha

Milwaukee

Detroit

Toronto

Lake Erie

Cleveland

New York

Chicago

Philadelphia

Kansas City

Indianapolis

Columbus

Cincinnati

WASHINGTON DC

Saint Louis

Ohio

Richmond

Norfolk

Wichita

Springfield

Louisville

Nashville

Raleigh

Oklahoma City

Memphis

Charlotte

ATLANTIC

Little Rock

Atlanta

Columbia

Dallas

Birmingham

Savannah

OCEAN

Austin

Jackson

Mobile

Jacksonville

⑫
▽

9

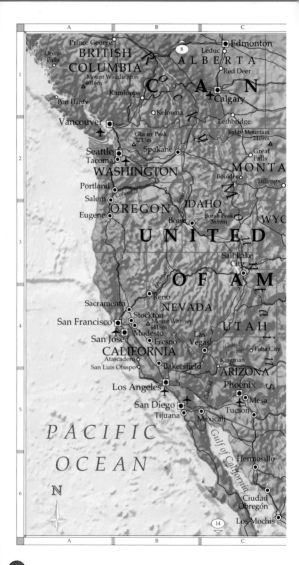

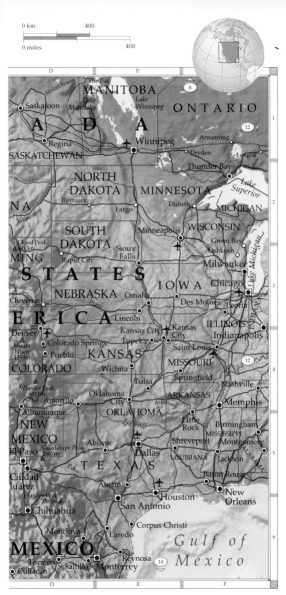

0 km   400

0 miles   400

MANITOBA

The Pas

Saskatchewan

Saskatoon

Lake Manitoba

Lake Winnipeg

O N T A R I O

8

A   **D**   **A**

Regina

Winnipeg

Armstrong

12

SASKATCHEWAN

Dryden

Longlac

Thunder Bay

NORTH DAKOTA

MINNESOTA

Lake Superior

N A

Bismarck

Yellowstone

Fargo

Duluth

MICHIGAN

SOUTH DAKOTA

Minneapolis

WISCONSIN

Green Bay

Oshkosh

Cloud Peak ▲4013m

MING

Rapid City

Sioux Falls

Missouri

Milwaukee

Lake Michigan

S T A T E S

IOWA

Chicago

NEBRASKA

Omaha

Des Moines

Peoria

Cheyenne

Platte

Lincoln

ILLINOIS

INDIANA

E R I C A

Kansas City

Kansas City

Indianapolis

Denver ▲

Mount Elbert 4399m

Colorado Springs

Topeka

Saint Louis

MISSOURI

12

Pueblo

KANSAS

COLORADO

Wichita

Beaver

Springfield

Nashville

Wheeler Peak 4011m

Tulsa

ARKANSAS

Memphis

Amarillo

Oklahoma City

Arkansas

Albuquerque

OKLAHOMA

Little Rock

Birmingham

NEW MEXICO

Red River

Shreveport

MISSISSIPPI

Montgomery

El Paso

Guadalupe Peak 2667m

Abilene

Dallas

LOUISIANA

Jackson

ALABAMA

Ciudad Juárez

Emory Peak 2385m ▲

T E X A S

Pecos

Baton Rouge

Chihuahua

Austin

Houston

New Orleans

San Antonio

Monclova

Corpus Christi

Laredo

Gulf of Mexico

MEXICO

Reynosa

14

Torreón

Saltillo

Monterrey

Culiacán

11

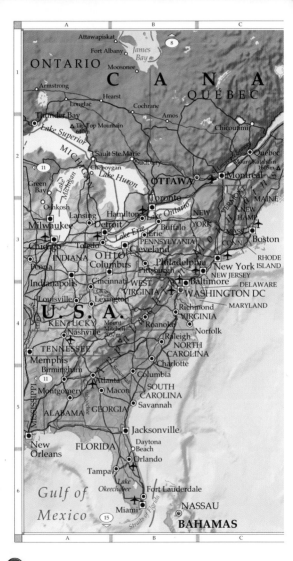

| 0 km | | 400 |
| 0 miles | | 400 |

NEWFOUNDLAND

AND

LABRADOR

○ St.Anthony

Newfoundland

*Gulf of
St. Lawrence*

Havre-St-Pierre

Ile d' Anticosti

○ Gander

Channel-Port aux
Basques

**St-Pierre
and Miquelon**
(to France)

⊕ ○ St.John's

NEW
BRUNSWICK

PRINCE
EDWARD
ISLAND

Moncton

*Grand Banks of
Newfoundland*

○ St.John

NOVA SCOTIA

⊕ Halifax

Sable Island

*Gulf
of
Maine*

● Hamilton

Bermuda
(to UK)

A T L A N T I C

O C E A N

N

13

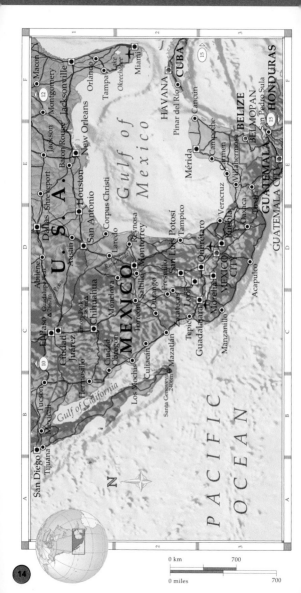

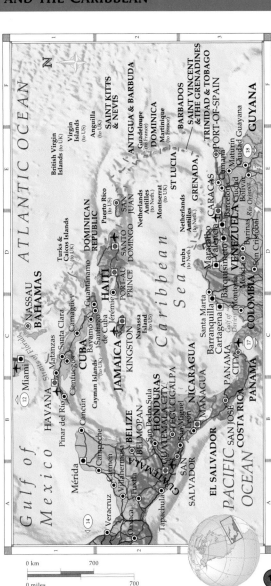

ATLANTIC OCEAN

Gulf of Mexico

Caribbean Sea

PACIFIC OCEAN

BAHAMAS
NASSAU

Miami
Florida
Pinar del Río
HAVANA
Matanzas
Cienfuegos
Santa Clara
CUBA
Camagüey
Bayamo
Santiago de Cuba
Cancún
Campeche
Mérida
Veracruz
Carmen
Villahermosa
Tuxtla
Oaxaca
Tapachula

Cayman Islands (to UK)

JAMAICA
KINGSTON

Navassa Island (to US)

HAITI
Jérémie
PORT-AU-PRINCE
Guantánamo

DOMINICAN REPUBLIC
SANTO DOMINGO
SAN JUAN
Puerto Rico (to US)

Turks & Caicos Islands (to UK)

British Virgin Islands (to UK)
Virgin Islands (to US)
Anguilla (to UK)

SAINT KITTS & NEVIS
ANTIGUA & BARBUDA
Guadeloupe (to France)
DOMINICA
Martinique (to France)
ST LUCIA
Netherlands Antilles (to Neth.)
Montserrat (to UK)

BARBADOS
SAINT VINCENT & THE GRENADINES
GRENADA
TRINIDAD & TOBAGO
PORT-OF-SPAIN

Netherlands Antilles (to Neth.)
Aruba (to Neth.)

Santa Marta
Barranquilla
Cartagena
Gulf of Darién
Montería
COLOMBIA
San Cristóbal

Maracaibo
Valencia
CARACAS
Cumaná
Barcelona
Maturín
Ciudad Guayana
Barquisimeto
Barinas
Mérida
VENEZUELA
Ciudad Bolívar
Río Orinoco

GUYANA

BELIZE
BELMOPAN
GUATEMALA
GUATEMALA CITY
San Pedro Sula
HONDURAS
TEGUCIGALPA
SAN SALVADOR
EL SALVADOR
San Miguel
León
MANAGUA
NICARAGUA
SAN JOSÉ
COSTA RICA
PANAMA
PANAMA CITY

0 km 700

0 miles 700

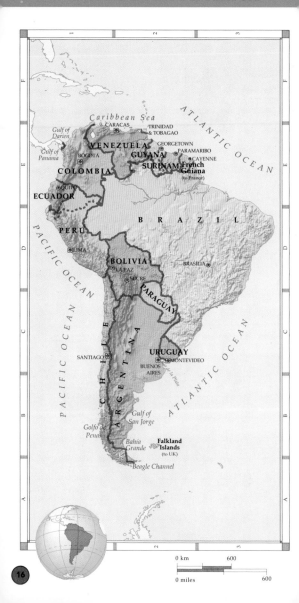

ATLANTIC OCEAN

Caribbean Sea

Gulf of Darien

CARACAS
TRINIDAD & TOBAGO

Gulf of Panama

VENEZUELA

GEORGETOWN

BOGOTÁ

GUYANA
PARAMARIBO

COLOMBIA

CAYENNE

SURINAM

French Guiana
(to France)

QUITO

ECUADOR

B R A Z I L

PERU

LIMA

BOLIVIA

BRASÍLIA

LA PAZ

SUCRE

PACIFIC OCEAN

PARAGUAY

C H I L E

URUGUAY

SANTIAGO

MONTEVIDEO

ARGENTINA

BUENOS AIRES

ATLANTIC OCEAN

Gulf of San Jorge

Golfo de Penas

Bahía Grande

Falkland Islands
(to UK)

Beagle Channel

0 km   600

0 miles   600

Caribbean Sea

HONDURAS
14
TEGUCIGALPA
NICARAGUA
Leon
MANAGUA

15

Netherlands
Antilles
Aruba (to Neth.)
(to Neth.)

COSTA RICA
SAN JOSÉ
PANAMA CITY
PANAMA

Santa Marta
Barranquilla
Cartagena
Montería
Gulf of Darien

Maracaibo
Valencia
VENEZUELA
Barquisimeto
Mérida
Cúcuta
San Cristóbal
Bucaramanga
Barinas

Gulf of Panama

Medellín

COLOMBIA
Armenia
Cali

BOGOTÁ
Villavicencio

Tunja
Río Meta

18

Equator
Galapagos
Islands

Esmeraldas

ECUADOR
Portoviejo
Babahoyo
Guayaquil
Gulf of Guayaquil
Machala

QUITO
Ambato
Riobamba
Cuenca

Neiva

Florencia

Pasto

Río Caquetá

Río Apaporis

Río Putumayo

Río Japurá

Iquitos

BRAZIL

Río Javari

Río Marañón

Piura
Bahía de Sechura
Chiclayo

Trujillo
Chimbote

PERU

Río Ucayali

Río Napo

Pucallpa

Río Juruá

18

N

Callao
LIMA
Ayacucho
Ica

Cusco

Nevado Papuya
6318m

Lake Titicaca

BOLIVIA

PACIFIC

OCEAN

Arequipa

Tacna
Arica

LA PAZ

Nevado Sajama
6520m

0 km   400
0 miles   400

17

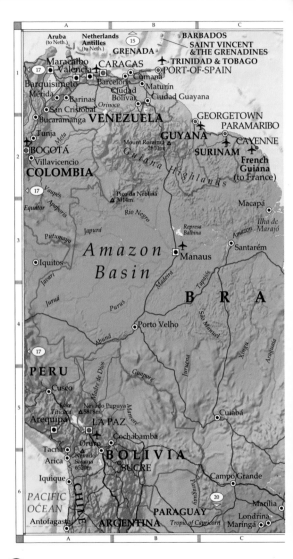

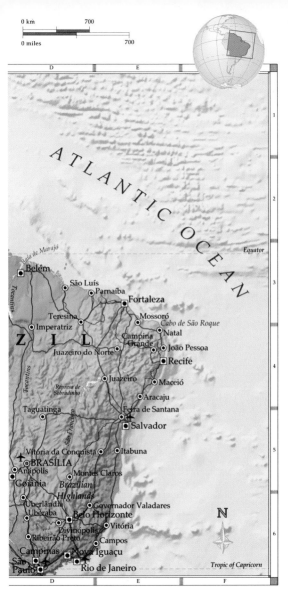

0 km 700

0 miles 700

ATLANTIC OCEAN

Baía de Marajó

Equator

Belém
São Luís
Parnaíba
Fortaleza
Teresina
Mossoró
Cabo de São Roque
Imperatriz
Natal
Campina Grande
João Pessoa
Juazeiro do Norte
Recife
Juazeiro
Maceió
Represa de Sobradinho
Aracaju
Taguatinga
Feira de Santana
Salvador
Vitória da Conquista
Itabuna
BRASÍLIA
Anápolis
Montes Claros
Goiânia
Brazilian Highlands
Uberlândia
Governador Valadares
Uberaba
Belo Horizonte
Divinópolis
Vitória
Ribeirão Preto
Campos
Campinas
Nova Iguaçu
São Paulo
Rio de Janeiro

Tocantins
Tocantins
São Francisco

Z   L   L

N

Tropic of Capricorn

D   E   F

19

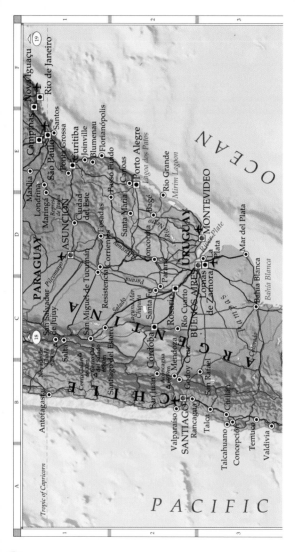

Nova Iguaçu
Rio de Janeiro
Campinas
São Paulo
Santos
Marília
Londrina
Curitiba
Maringá
Joinville
Ponta Grossa
Blumenau
Florianópolis
Ciudad del Este
Passo Fundo
Caxias
Porto Alegre
Lagoa dos Patos
Santa Maria
Posadas
Rio Grande
Bagé
Mirim Lagoon
Concordia
Corrientes
MONTEVIDEO
Resistencia
Paraná
URUGUAY
Paraná
Santa Fe
San Miguel de Tucumán
Mar del Plata
Laguna Mar Chiquita
Santiago del Estero
Rosario
Río Cuarto
BUENOS AIRES
Lomas de Zamora
La Plata
Río de la Plata
Córdoba
Bahía Blanca
Bahía Blanca
Mendoza
Godoy Cruz
San Juan
San Rafael
Aconcagua 6960m
Cerro Tupungato 6550m
Valparaíso
SANTIAGO
Rancagua
Talca
Chillán
Concepción
Talcahuano
Temuco
Valdivia

PARAGUAY
ASUNCIÓN
San Salvador de Jujuy
Salta
Nevado de Chañi 6030m
Antofagasta

CHILE
ARGENTINA

Pilcomayo
Salado
Río Dulce
Salado del Salado

Tropic of Capricorn

PACIFIC OCEAN

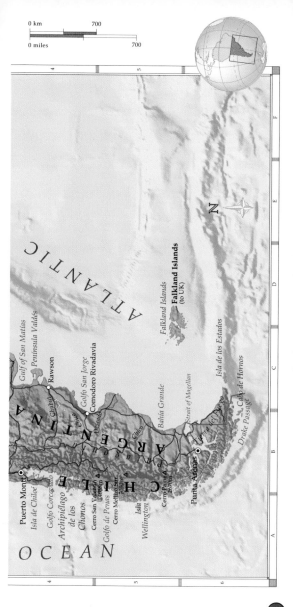

0 km 700

0 miles 700

N

ATLANTIC

OCEAN

Falkland Islands
Falkland Islands
(to UK)

Isla de los Estados

Cabo de Hornos

Drake Passage

Strait of Magellan

Bahía Grande

Tierra del Fuego

Punta Arenas

Cerro Paine ▲
2670m

Isla
Wellington

Cerro Melimoyu Sur ▲
2350m

Cerro de Penas

Golfo de Penas

Cerro San Valentín ▲
4058m

Archipiélago
de los
Chonos

Golfo Corcovado

Isla de Chiloé

Puerto Montt

C H I L E

A R G E N T I N A

Golfo San Jorge

Comodoro Rivadavia

Deseado

Chubut

Rawson

Gulf of San Matías

Península Valdés

Chico

21

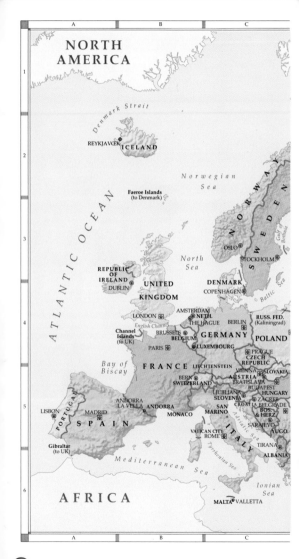

Kara
Sea

Barents
Sea

ASIA

White
Sea

RUSSIAN

FINLAND

FEDERATION

HELSINKI

TALLINN

ESTONIA

LATVIA

RIGA

MOSCOW

LITHUANIA

VILNIUS

MINSK

BELORUSSIA

WARSAW

KIEV

UKRAINE

MOLDAVIA

CHISINCU

Sea of
Azov

Caspian Sea

ROMANIA

BUCHAREST

Black Sea

BULGARIA

SOFIA

SKOPJE

MACEDONIA

TURKEY

ASIA

Aegean
Sea

GREECE

ATHENS

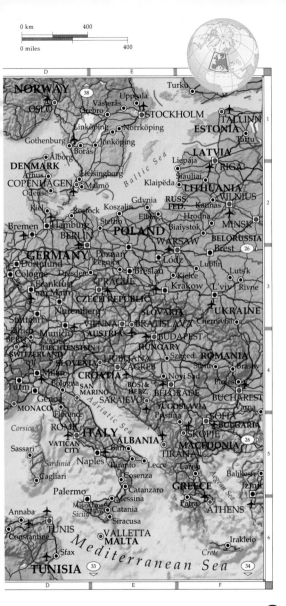

0 km   400
0 miles   400

D   **E**

38

Solikamsk • • Serov

FEDERATION   Kirov • Glazov • Perm' •

• Kineshma   Izhevsk • Yekaterinburg •

Volga Nizhniy Novgorod   Naberezhnyye Chelny

• Kazan'   Ufa • Chelyabinsk •

Ul'yanovsk   Sterlitamak •

Tol'yatti

• Tambov   • Penza   Samara   Magnitogorsk •

• Balakovo

Saratov   Ural'sk •   Orenburg • Orsk •

Don   Aktyubinsk •   38

Volgograd

KAZAKHSTAN

• Stavropol'   Astrakhan'   *Ustyurt* *Aral*
Plateau *Sea*

• Nal'chik • Grozhyy   Aktau •
Makhachkala   *Caspian*   **UZBEKISTAN**
• Sokhumi   *Sea*   • Nukus

GEORGIA T'BILISI   Dashkhovuz •

• Batumi   Ganca   **AZERBAIJAN**   **TURKMENISTAN**

ARMENIA YEREVAN   BAKU

Mount Ararat   Khvoy •
5137m   **ASHGABAT**
• Van   Tabriz •   Gora Chapan
Lake   2889m
Urmia   Rasht •   • Gorgan   Mashhad •
• Mosul   Zanjan •   TEHRAN   Sabzevar •
• Kirkuk   • Sanandaj   • Qom   **I R A N**   Herat •
IRAQ

BAGHDAD   Bakhtaran •   • Kashan   34

D   **E**   **F**

27

POLITICAL AFRICA

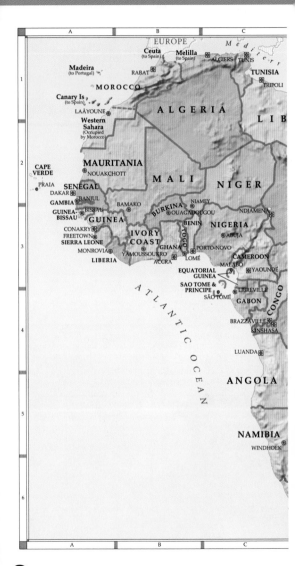

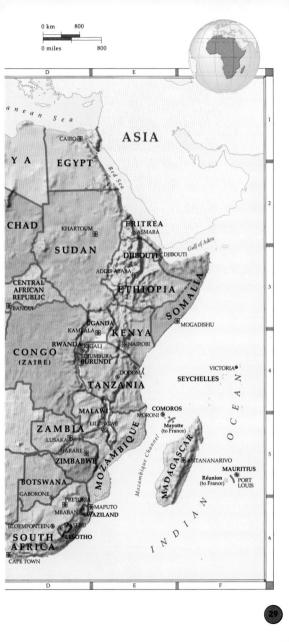

0 km   800

0 miles   800

anean Sea

ASIA

CAIRO ⊕

Y A

EGYPT

Red Sea

CHAD

KHARTOUM ⊕

ERITREA
⊕ ASMARA

Gulf of Aden

SUDAN

DJIBOUTI ⊕ DJIBOUTI

ADDIS ABABA ⊕

CENTRAL
AFRICAN
REPUBLIC

ETHIOPIA

SOMALIA

⊙ BANGUI

UGANDA
KAMPALA ⊕

KENYA

MOGADISHU

RWANDA ⊙ KIGALI

⊕ NAIROBI

CONGO
(ZAIRE)

BUJUMBURA
BURUNDI

VICTORIA ●

DODOMA ⊕

SEYCHELLES

TANZANIA

O
C
E
A
N

MALAWI

COMOROS
MORONI ⊕

ZAMBIA

LILONGWE ⊕

Mayotte
(to France)

LUSAKA ⊙

HARARE ⊙

ZIMBABWE

Mozambique Channel

ANTANANARIVO ⊙

MAURITIUS

BOTSWANA

Réunion
(to France)

⊙ PORT
LOUIS

GABORONE ⊙

PRETORIA ⊙

MADAGASCAR

MAPUTO

BLOEMFONTEIN ⊙

MBABANE ⊙ SWAZILAND

⊙ MASERU

SOUTH
AFRICA

LESOTHO

I
N
D
I
A
N

⊕ CAPE TOWN

SOUTHERN AFRICA

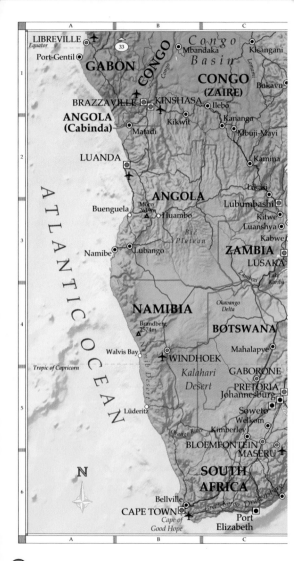

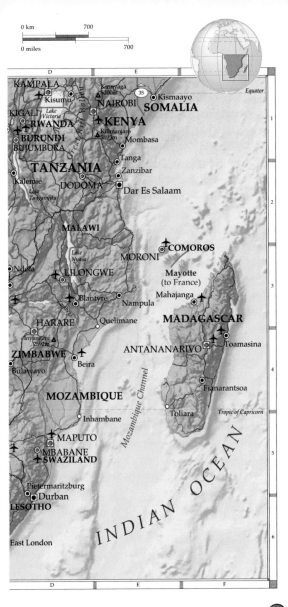

KAMPALA

Kisumu

Kirinyaga
5200m

NAIROBI

SOMALIA

Kismaayo

Equator

KIGALI

Lake
Victoria

RWANDA

BURUNDI

Mombasa

KENYA

Kilimanjaro
5895m

BUJUMBURA

Great Rift Valley

TANZANIA

Tanga

Kalemie

DODOMA

Zanzibar

Dar Es Salaam

Lake
Tanganyika

MALAWI

Lake
Nyasa

COMOROS

Ndola

LILONGWE

MORONI

Mayotte
(to France)

Blantyre

Nampula

Mahajanga

HARARE

Quelimane

MADAGASCAR

Inyangani
2592m

ANTANANARIVO

Toamasina

ZIMBABWE

Beira

Bulawayo

Fianarantsoa

MOZAMBIQUE

Mozambique Channel

Toliara

Tropic of Capricorn

Inhambane

MAPUTO

MBABANE

SWAZILAND

Pietermaritzburg

Durban

LESOTHO

East London

INDIAN OCEAN

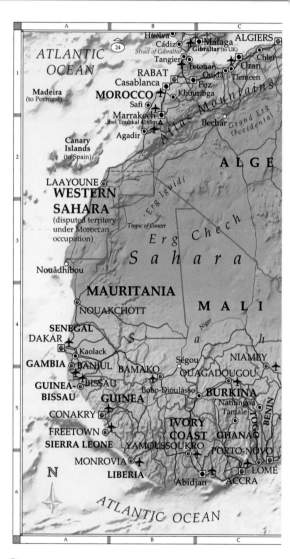

ATLANTIC OCEAN

Huelva
Cádiz
Strait of Gibraltar
Tangier
Málaga ALGIERS
Gibraltar (to UK)
Tetouan
Oujda
Oran
Chlef
Tlemcen
Casablanca
RABAT
MOROCCO
Khouribga
Fez
Madeira
(to Portugal)
Safi
Marrakech
Jbel Toubkal 4165m
Bechar
Grand Erg Occidental
Agadir
Atlas Mountains

Canary Islands
(to Spain)

ALGE

LAAYOUNE
WESTERN
SAHARA
(disputed territory
under Moroccan
occupation)

Erg Iguidi

Tropic of Cancer
Erg Chech
Sahara

Nouâdhibou

MAURITANIA
NOUAKCHOTT

MALI

Niger

SENEGAL
DAKAR

S   a   h

Kaolack
Ségou
NIAMEY
GAMBIA
BANJUL
BAMAKO
OUAGADOUGOU
GUINEA-
BISSAU
BISSAU
Bobo-Dioulasso
BURKINA
GUINEA
Natitingou
Tamale
CONAKRY
FREETOWN
IVORY
COAST
GHANA
SIERRA LEONE
YAMOUSSOUKRO
PORTO-NOVO
MONROVIA
LOMÉ
LIBERIA
Abidjan
ACCRA

N

ATLANTIC OCEAN

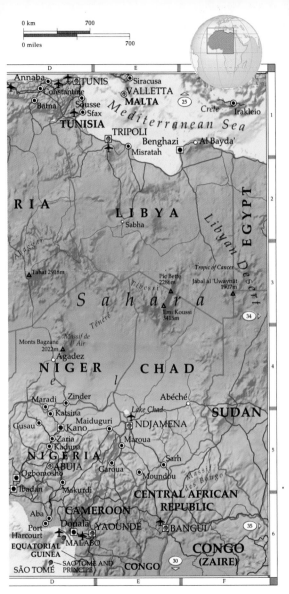

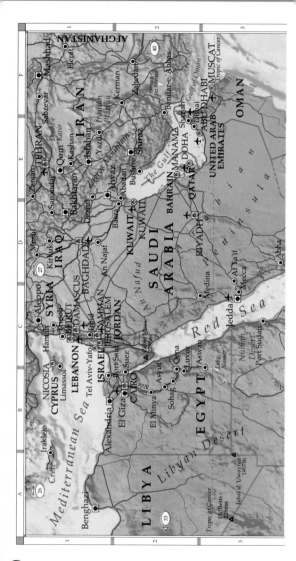

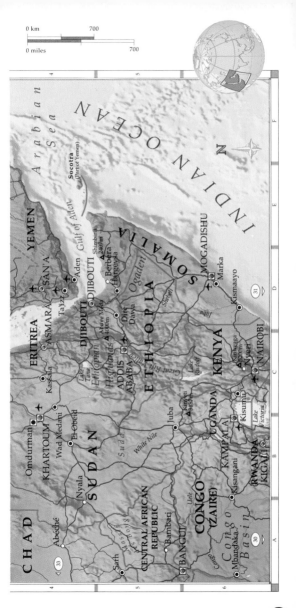

0 km 700
0 miles 700

N

Arabian Sea

INDIAN OCEAN

Socotra
(Part of Yemen)

Gulf of Aden

YEMEN
SAN'A
Aden

ERITREA
ASMARA
Taʿizz
Kassala

DJIBOUTI
DJIBOUTI
Dire Dawa
Berbera
Hargeysa

Shimbiris
△2467m

SOMALIA
MOGADISHU
Marka
Kismaayo

Ogaden

Shebeli

Juba

Abuye Meda
△4000m
Ethiopian
Highlands
Lake Tana
ADDIS ABABA

ETHIOPIA

Great Rift Valley

Lake Turkana

KENYA
NAIROBI
Kirinyaga
△5200m
Nyeri

Kanyeti
△3185m

Omdurman
KHARTOUM
Wad Medani
El-Obeid

SUDAN

Nyala

White Nile

Sudd

UGANDA
KAMPALA
Kisumu
Lake Victoria

RWANDA
KIGALI

Abeché

CHAD

Sarh

Nyala

CENTRAL AFRICAN REPUBLIC
Bambari
BANGUI

Massif des Bongo

Mbandaka

CONGO
(ZAIRE)
Kisangani

Congo Basin

Uele

Uba ngi

Lomami

Congo

30

31

33

35

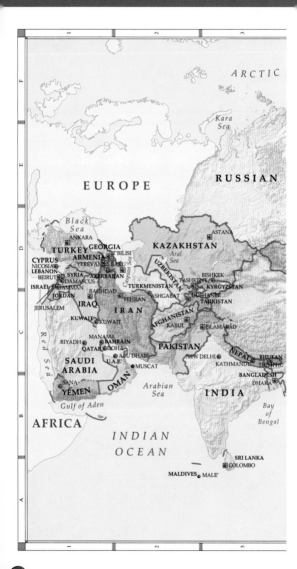

ARCTIC

Kara Sea

EUROPE   RUSSIAN

ASTANA

Black Sea

ANKARA

KAZAKHSTAN

TURKEY GEORGIA
                T'BILISI   *Aral Sea*
CYPRUS ARMENIA
NICOSIA   YEREVAN BAKU   UZBEKISTAN
LEBANON   BISHKEK
BEIRUT SYRIA   AZERBAIJAN   TASHKENT
ISRAEL DAMASCUS   *Caspian Sea*   KYRGYZSTAN
        AMMAN   TURKMENISTAN DUSHANBE
JORDAN   BAGHDAD   ASHGABAT   TAJIKISTAN
JERUSALEM   TEHRAN
          IRAQ   IRAN   AFGHANISTAN
KUWAIT   KABUL   ISLAMABAD
        KUWAIT
                                              PAKISTAN   NEPAL
        RIYADH   MANAMA BAHRAIN   BHUTAN
                 QATAR DOHA   NEW DELHI KATHMANDU THIMPHU
SAUDI   U.A.E. ABU DHABI   BANGLADESH
ARABIA   MUSCAT   DHAKA
        SANA'   OMAN   *Arabian Sea*
        YEMEN   INDIA
Red Sea   *Gulf of Aden*

AFRICA   *Bay of Bengal*

INDIAN OCEAN

                                        SRI LANKA
                                        COLOMBO

                        MALDIVES MALE'

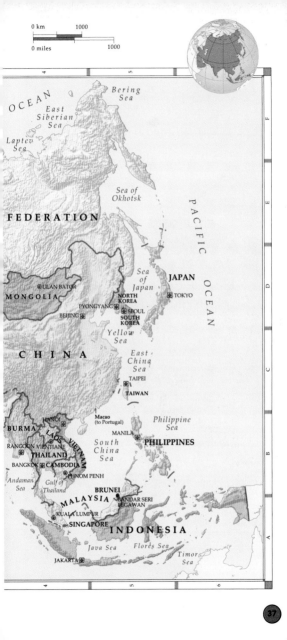

0 km   1000

0 miles   1000

OCEAN

East Siberian Sea

Bering Sea

Laptev Sea

FEDERATION

Sea of Okhotsk

PACIFIC OCEAN

◉ULAN BATOR

MONGOLIA

Sea of Japan

JAPAN

◉ TOKYO

NORTH KOREA

PYONGYANG◉   ◉SEOUL
             SOUTH
BEIJING◉   KOREA

Yellow Sea

C H I N A

East China Sea

TAIPEI

TAIWAN

Macao
(to Portugal)

Philippine Sea

BURMA   LAOS   HANOI
              VIETNAM

RANGOON◉ VIENTIANE◉   MANILA

THAILAND

South China Sea

PHILIPPINES

BANGKOK◉ ◉CAMBODIA

◉PHNOM PENH

Andaman Sea

Gulf of Thailand

BRUNEI

MALAYSIA   ◉BANDAR SERI
                BEGAWAN

◉KUALA LUMPUR

◉SINGAPORE

INDONESIA

Java Sea   *Flores Sea*

Timor Sea

JAKARTA◉

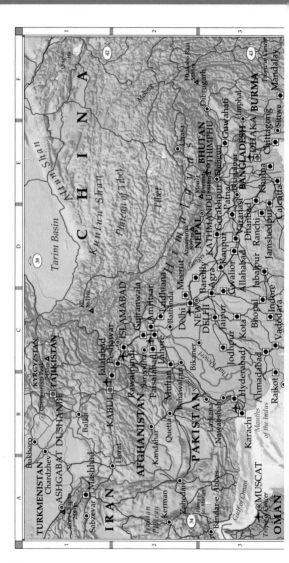

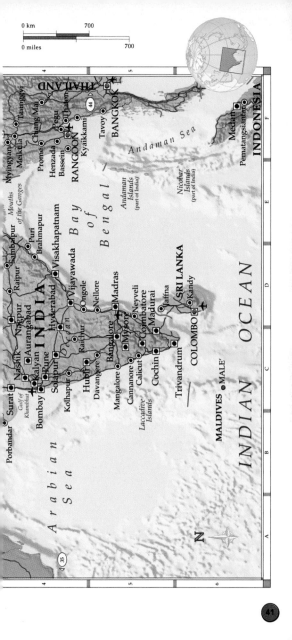

0 km 700

0 miles 700

THAILAND

Taungyi

Myingyan

Meiktila

Chiang Mai

Pegu

Prome

Henzada

Bassein

RANGOON

Tavoy

Kyaikkami

BANGKOK

Chon

Andaman Sea

Mouths
of the Ganges

Jamshedpur

Raipur

Puri

Brahmapur

Visakhapatnam

Bay
of
Bengal

Andaman
Islands
(part of India)

Nicobar
Islands
(part of India)

Medan

Pematangsiantar

INDONESIA

Nagpur

Aurangabad

Vijayawada

Hyderabad

Madras

SRI LANKA

Surat

Nashik

Kalyan

Bombay

Pune

Solapur

Raichur

Ongole

Nellore

Neyveli

Coimbatore

Jaffna

Kandy

Porbandar

Gulf of
Khambhat

D e c c a n

Hubli

Bangalore

Mysore

Madurai

COLOMBO

Kolhapur

Davangere

Mangalore

Cannanore

Calicut

Cochin

Trivandrum

INDIA

Raichur

Laccadive
Islands

MALDIVES ● MALE

A r a b i a n
S e a

INDIAN OCEAN

N

35

41

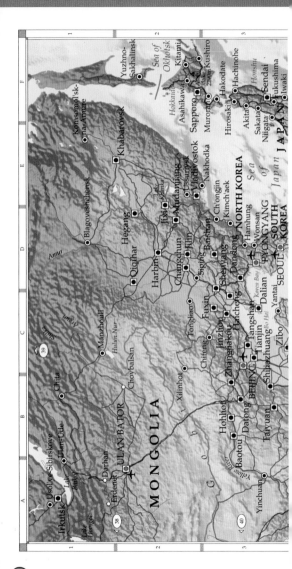

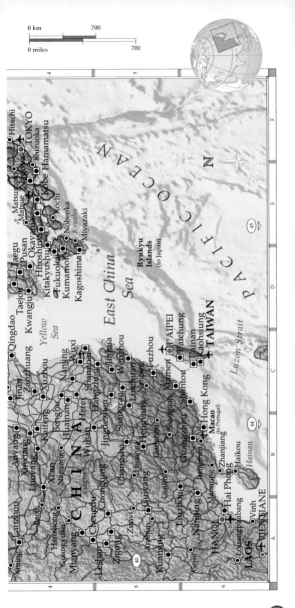

0 km 700
0 miles 700

PACIFIC OCEAN

East China Sea

Yellow Sea

Ryukyu Islands (to Japan)

Luzon Strait

N

Hitachi
TOKYO
Shizuoka
Nagoya
Matsumoto
Matsue
Kobe
Hamamatsu
Okayama
Kochi
Hiroshima
Nobeoka
Kitakyushu
Miyazaki
Fukuoka
Kumamoto
Kagoshima
Kyushu
Taegu
Taejon
Pusan
Kwangju

Qingdao
Jinan
Zaozhuang
Xuzhou
Nanjing
Wuxi
Shanghai
Hangzhou
Ningbo
Wenzhou
Linhai
Jinhua
Fuzhou
TAIPEI
Taichung
Xiamen
Shantou
Kaohsiung
Tainan
TAIWAN

Anyang
Xinxiang
Luoyang
Kaifeng
Bengbu
Huainan
Hefei
Wuhan
Jingdezhen
Shangrao
Nanchang
Ji'an
Shaoguan
Guangzhou
Hong Kong
Macao (to Portugal)

C H I N A

Xining
Lanzhou
Baoji
Xi'an
Nanyang
Hanzhong
Guangyuan
Mianyang
Chengdu
Leshan
Zigong
Neijiang
Chongqing
Zunyi
Guiyang
Guilin
Liuzhou
Nanning
Gejiu
Kunming
Yangtze
Mekong

Changsha
Huaihua
Hengyang
Zhuzhou

Zhanjiang
Haikou
Jiangmen
Hainan

LAOS
Louangphabang
VIENTIANE
Vinh
Hai Phong
HANOI
Vinh

45

44

40

43

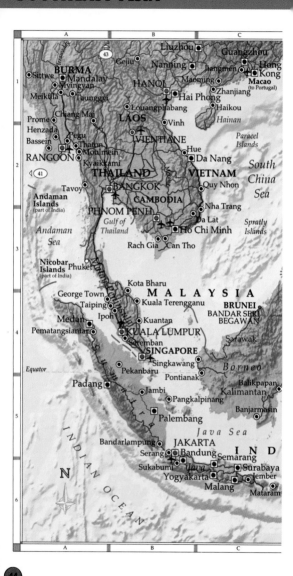

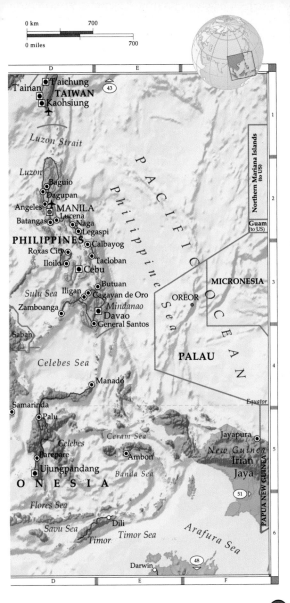

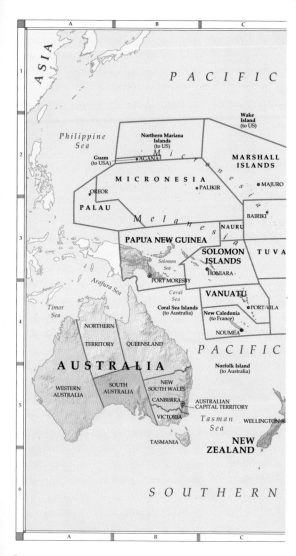

ASIA

PACIFIC

Philippine Sea

Northern Mariana Islands (to US)

Wake Island (to US)

MARSHALL ISLANDS

Guam (to USA) ●AGANA

Micronesia

MICRONESIA ●PALIKIR

●MAJURO

OREOR●

PALAU

Melanesia

BAIRIKI●

NAURU

PAPUA NEW GUINEA

Solomon Sea

SOLOMON ISLANDS

TUVA

●PORT MORESBY

HONIARA●

Arafura Sea

Coral Sea

VANUATU

●PORT-VILA

Timor Sea

Coral Sea Islands (to Australia)

New Caledonia (to France)

NORTHERN

NOUMEA●

TERRITORY

QUEENSLAND

PACIFIC

AUSTRALIA

Norfolk Island (to Australia)

WESTERN AUSTRALIA

SOUTH AUSTRALIA

NEW SOUTH WALES

CANBERRA●

AUSTRALIAN CAPITAL TERRITORY

VICTORIA

Tasman Sea

WELLINGTON●

TASMANIA

NEW ZEALAND

SOUTHERN

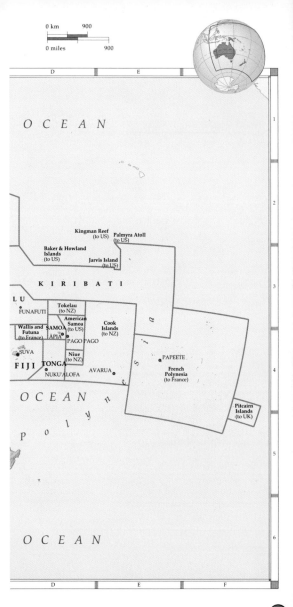

0 km   900

0 miles   900

OCEAN

Kingman Reef
(to US)   Palmyra Atoll
(to US)

Baker & Howland
Islands
(to US)

Jarvis Island
(to US)

K I R I B A T I

L U

FUNAFUTI

Tokelau
(to NZ)

American
Samoa
(to US)

Cook
Islands
(to NZ)

Wallis and
Futuna
(to France)

SAMOA

APIA

PAGO PAGO

SUVA

Niue
(to NZ)

FIJI

TONGA

NUKU'ALOFA

AVARUA

PAPEETE

French
Polynesia
(to France)

OCEAN

P o l y n e s i a

Pitcairn
Islands
(to UK)

OCEAN

AUSTRALIA

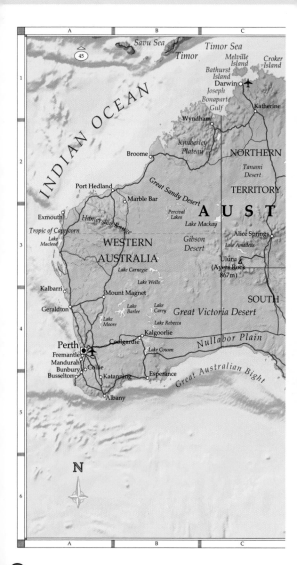

Savu Sea

Timor

Timor Sea

INDIAN OCEAN

45

Melville Island

Croker Island

Bathurst Island

Darwin

Joseph Bonaparte Gulf

Katherine

Wyndham

NORTHERN

Kimberley Plateau

Broome

Tanami Desert

TERRITORY

Port Hedland

Great Sandy Desert

Marble Bar

Percival Lakes

Lake Mackay

A U S T

Exmouth

Hamersley Range

Tropic of Capricorn

Lake Macleod

WESTERN

Gibson Desert

Alice Springs

Lake Amadeus

Uluru (Ayers Rock) 867m)

AUSTRALIA

Kalbarri

Lake Carnegie

Lake Wells

SOUTH

Geraldton

Mount Magnet

Lake Barlee

Lake Carey

Great Victoria Desert

Lake Moore

Lake Rebecca

Perth

Kalgoorlie

Fremantle

Coolgardie

Nullarbor Plain

Mandurah

Lake Cowan

Bunbury

Collie

Busselton

Katanning

Esperance

Great Australian Bight

Albany

N

48

0 km   700

0 miles   700

PAPUA NEW GUINEA

● PORT
  MORESBY

**SOLOMON
ISLANDS**

*Arafura
Sea*

Torres Strait

*Wessel
Islands*

*Cape
York
Peninsula*

50

*Coral
Sea*

VANUATU

**Gulf of
Carpentaria**

● Cairns

50

Great Barrier Reef

New Caledonia
(to France)

○ Townsville
Bowen

**Coral Sea
Islands**
(to Australia)

● Cloncurry

Mount Isa

○ Mackay

R A L I A

PACIFIC OCEAN

Longreach

Rockhampton
● Gladstone

QUEENSLAND

Bundaberg
Maryborough
Gympie
Caloundra

*Simpson
Desert*

Charleville

Toowoomba ○□ **Brisbane**
Ipswich ● Surfers Paradise

AUSTRALIA

Moree

**NEW SOUTH
WALES**

Grafton

Armidale
Tamworth

Coffs Harbour

Port Macquarie

Darling

Dubbo

Taree

*Lake
Gairdner*

□ Port Augusta
Broken Hill

Parkes
Orange
Bathurst

Newcastle

Whyalla
Port Pirie

Mildura

● **Sydney**
□ Wollongong

*Port
Lincoln*

✛ **Adelaide**

Wagga Wagga

Goulburn

□● **CANBERRA**

*Kangaroo
Island*

VICTORIA

Bendigo

Wangaratta

**AUSTRALIAN
CAPITAL TERRITORY**

Mount Gambier ● Ballarat

□● **Melbourne**

Traralgon

Portland
Warrnambool

Geelong

King Island

51

Bass Strait

Hunter Island

Burnie
Devonport ● Launceston

TASMANIA

*T a s m a n
Sea*

● **Hobart**

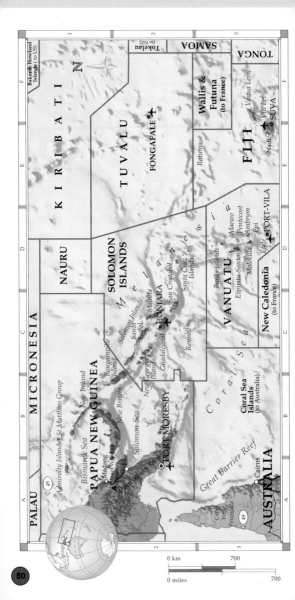

NEW ZEALAND AND SOUTHEAST AUSTRALIA

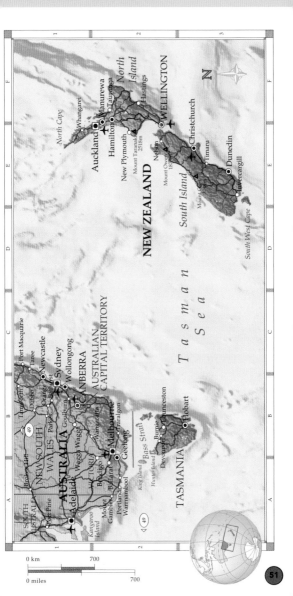

North Cape

Whangarei

Auckland
Manurewa
Hamilton
Tauranga
North
Island
Hastings
New Plymouth
Mount Taranaki
2518m
WELLINGTON

NEW ZEALAND

N

Nelson
Mount Owen
Mount Cook
Christchurch
Timaru
Dunedin
Invercargill
South Island
South West Cape

Tasman Sea

Port Macquarie
Taree
Newcastle
Sydney
Wollongong
CANBERRA
AUSTRALIAN
CAPITAL TERRITORY

Tamworth
Dubbo
Orange
Bathurst
Parkes
Goulburn
NEW SOUTH
WALES

AUSTRALIA

Broken Hill
49
Adelaide
Port Pirie
Mount
Gambier
Kangaroo
Island
SOUTH
AUSTRALIA

Wagga Wagga
Wangaratta
Shepparton
Bendigo
Ballarat
Melbourne
Geelong
Portland
Warrnambool

Launceston
Burnie
Devonport
Hobart
TASMANIA
King Island
Hunter Island
Bass Strait

49

0 km   700

0 miles   700

51

THE ARCTIC

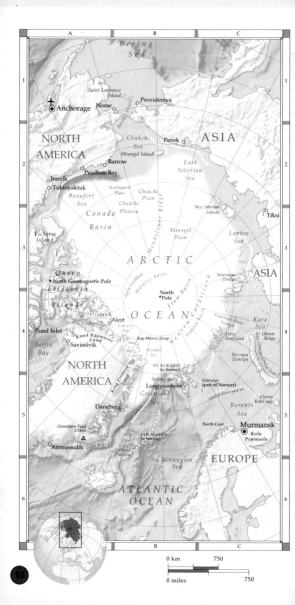

Bering Sea

Saint Lawrence Island

✈ Anchorage
Nome
Providenya

NORTH
AMERICA

ASIA

Chukchi Sea
Pevek

Wrangel Island

Barrow
Prudhoe Bay

Inuvik
Tuktoyaktuk

East Siberian Sea

Beaufort Sea

Northwind Plain
Chukchi Plain
Chukchi Plateau

New Siberian Islands

Tiksi

Canada Basin

Mendeleyev Ridge

Wrangel Plain

Laptev Sea

Victoria Island

ARCTIC

Queen
Elizabeth
Islands

North Geomagnetic Pole

Alpha Cordillera

Makarov Basin

North Pole

Fram Basin

Severnaya Zemlya

ASIA

Lomonosov Ridge

Nansen Cordillera

Nansen Basin

Kara Sea

Ostrov Belyy

Ellesmere Island

OCEAN

Alert
Lincoln Sea

Kap Morris Jesup

Pond Inlet

Knud Rasmussen Land
Savissivik

Baffin Bay

Wandel Sea

Land of Frederik VIII

SVALBARD
(to Norway)

Spitsbergen
Longyearbyen

Bjørnøya
(part of Norway)

Greenland Sea

Franz Josef Land

Novaya Zemlya

Kara white sea ice

Ostrov Kotel'nyy

Scoresby Anna Trench

NORTH
AMERICA

Daneborg

Gunnbjørn Fjeld 3700m △

JAN MAYEN
(to Norway)

North Cape

Murmansk
Kola Peninsula

Barents Sea

Ammassalik

Denmark Strait

Iceland Plateau

Norwegian Sea

EUROPE

ATLANTIC
OCEAN

B   C

0 km   750

0 miles   750

ANTARCTICA

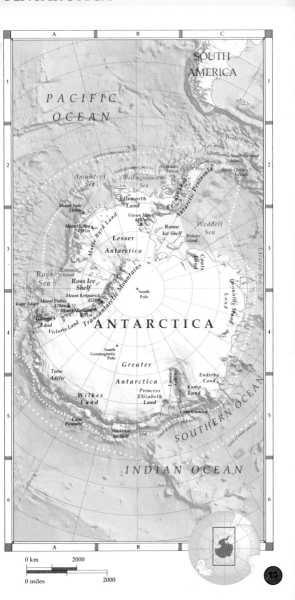

SOUTH
AMERICA

PACIFIC
OCEAN

Drake Passage

Limit of winter pack ice

Limit of summer pack ice

South Shetland
Islands

Amundsen
Sea

Bellingshausen
Sea

Alexander
Island

South Orkney
Islands

Ellsworth
Land

Palmer Land

Antarctic Peninsula

Mount Siple
3100m ▲

Vinson Massif
4897m ▲

Ronne
Ice Shelf

Weddell
Sea

Mount Sidley ▲
4181m

Lesser
Antarctica

Berkner
Island

Coats
Land

Marie Byrd Land

Roosevelt
Island

Ross Ice
Shelf

Mount Kirkpatrick
4528m ▲

South
Pole
+

Dronning Maud
Land

Ross
Sea

Cape Adare

Mount Erebus
3794m ▲

Mount Markham ▲
4351m

Transantarctic Mountains

ANTARCTICA

Lützow-Holm
Bay

George V
Land

Victoria Land

South
Geomagnetic
Pole +

Greater
Antarctica

Enderby
Land

Terre
Adélie

Lambert Glacier

Kemp
Land

Wilkes
Land

Princess
Elizabeth
Land

Mackenzie
Bay

Cape Darnley

Cape
Poinsett

Shackleton
Ice Shelf

Davis
Sea

Prydz Bay

Limit of summer pack ice

SOUTHERN OCEAN

Limit of winter pack ice

INDIAN OCEAN

0 km   2000

0 miles   2000

53

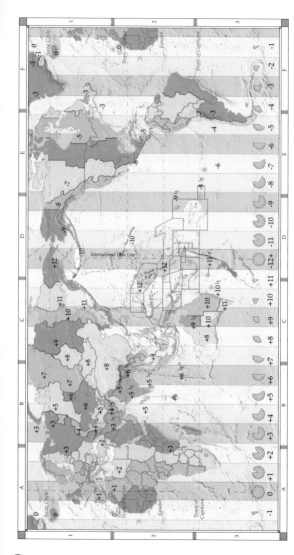

INDEX

Armenia *Country* SW Asia 27 D5

Armidale NSW, SE Australia 49 E4

Armstrong Ontario, S Canada ⁹11 F1

Arnhem Land *Physical region* Northern Territory, N Australia 3 C3

Aruba *Dutch autonomous region* S Caribbean Sea 15 D2

Asaþi-dake *Mountain* N Japan 42 F2

Asahikawa N Japan 42 F2

Ashgabat *Country capital* C Turkmenistan 27 F5

Asia *Continent* 3 B1

Asmara *Country capital* C Eritrea 35 C4

Astana N Kazakhstan 38 B4

Astrakhan' SW Russ. Fed. 27 E4

Asunción *Country capital* S Paraguay 20 D1

Aswan SE Egypt 34 B3

Asyut C Egypt 34 B2

At Ta'if W Saudi Arabia 34 D3

Atascadero California, USA 10 A4

Athabasca, Lake *Lake* Alberta / Saskatchewan, SW Canada 8 C4

Athens *Country capital* C Greece 26 A5

Atlanta Georgia, USA 12 A5

Atlantic Ocean 3 F2

Atlas Mountains *Mountain range* NW Africa 32 C1

Attawapiskat Ontario, C Canada 12 B1

Auckland North Island, NZ 51 E2

Aurangabad C India 41 C4

Austin Texas, USA 11 E5

Australia *Country* Oceana 48 B3

Australian Capital Territory *Territory* SE Australia 49 E5

Austria *Country* C Europe 25 E4

Avarua *Country capital* C Solomon Islands 47 E4

Aydın SW Turkey 26 B6

Azerbaijan *Country* SE Asia 27 D5

B

Badajoz W Spain 24 B5

Baffin Bay *Bay* Canada / Greenland 9 E3

Baffin Island *Island* NW Terr., NE Canada 9 D3

Bagé S Brazil 20 D2

Baghdad *Country capital* N Iraq 34 D1

Baguio N Philippines 45 D2

Bagzane, Monts *Mountain* N Niger 33 D4

Bahamas *Country* N West Indies 15 C1

Bahawalpur E Pakistan 40 B2

Bahía Blanca E Argentina 20 C3

Bahrain *Country* SW Asia 34 E2

Baikal, Lake *Lake* Russian Federation 3 C1

Bairiki *Country capital* Tarawa, NW Kiribati 46 C3

Baishan NE China 42 D3

Baja California *Peninsula* NW Mexico 3 E2

Baker & Howland Islands *Country* W Pacific Ocean 47 D3

Bakersfield California, USA 10 B4

Bakhtaran W Iran 34 D1

Baku *Country capital* E Azerbaijan 27 D5

Balakovo SW Russ. Fed. 27 D3

Balbina, Represa *Reservoir* NW Brazil 18 B3

Baldy Mountain *Mountain* Montana, USA 10 C2

Balearic Islands *Island group* Spain, W Mediterranean Sea 24 C5

Balıkesir W Turkey 26 B5

Balikpapan C Indonesia 44 C5

Balkh N Afghanistan 40 B1

Balkhash SE Kazakhstan 38 B5

Balkhash, Lake *Lake* SE Kazakhstan 38 B5

Ballarat Victoria, SE Australia 49 E5

Baltic Sea *Sea* N Europe 25 E2

Baltimore Maryland, USA 12 B4

Bamako *Country capital* SW Mali 32 B5

Bambari C CAR 35 A5

Banda Sea *Sea* E Indonesia 45 E5

Bandar Seri Begawan *Country capital* N Brunei 44 C4

Bandar-e 'Abbas S Iran 34 F2

Bandarlampung Sumatra, W Indonesia 44 B5

Bandung Java, C Indonesia 44 B5

Bangalore S India 41 C5

Bangkok *Country capital* C Thailand 44 A2

Bangladesh *Country* S Asia 40 E3

Bangui *Country capital* SW CAR 33 E6

Banjarmasin C Indonesia 44 C5

Banjul *Country capital* W Gambia 32 A4

Banks Islands *Island group* N Vanuatu 50 D3

Baoji C China 43 A4

Baotou N China 42 A3

Barbados *Country* SE West Indies 15 E2

Barcelona E Spain 24 C5

Barcelona NE Venezuela 18 A1

Bareilly N India 40 C3

Barents Sea *Sea* Arctic Ocean 38 B2

Bari SE Italy 25 E5

Barinas W Venezuela 18 A1

Barlee, Lake *Lake* Western Australia 48 B4

Barquisimeto NW Venezuela 18 A1

Barranquilla N Colombia 15 C3

Barrow Alaska, USA 52 A2

Basra SE Iraq 34 D2

Bass Strait *Strait* SE Australia 51 B2

Bassein SW Burma 41 F4

Bat'umi W Georgia 27 D5

Batangas N Philippines 45 D2

Bathinda NW India 40 C2

Bathurst Island *Island* Northern Territory, N Australia 48 C1

Bathurst NSW, SE Australia 49 E5

Batna NE Algeria 33 D1

Baton Rouge Louisiana, USA 11 F5

Bayamo E Cuba 15 C1

Beaufort Sea *Sea* Arctic Ocean 8 C2

Beaver River *River* Oklahoma, USA 11 E4

Bechar W Algeria 32 C2

Beijing *Country capital* E China 42 B3

Beira C Mozambique 31 D4

Beirut *Country capital* W Lebanon 34 C1

Belém N Brazil 19 D3

Belfast *Political division capital* E Northern Ireland, UK 24 B2

Belgium *Country* NW Europe 24 C3

Belgorod W Russ. Fed. 26 C3

Belgrade *Country capital* N Yugoslavia 25 E4

Belize *Country* Central America 15 B2

Bellingshausen Sea *Sea* Antarctica 53 B2

Bellville SW South Africa 30 B6

Belmopan *Country capital* C Belize 15 B2

Belo Horizonte SE Brazil 19 D6

Belorussia *Country* E Europe 26 A2

Belyy, Ostrov *Island* N Russ. Fed. 52 C4

Ben Nevis *Mountain* N Scotland, UK 24 B2

Bendigo Victoria, SE Australia 49 E5

Bengal, Bay of *Bay* N Indian Ocean 41 E5

Bengbu E China 43 C4

Benghazi NE Libya 33 E1

Benguela W Angola 30 B3

Benin *Country* W Africa 32 C5

Berbera NW Somalia 35 D5

Bergen S Norway 24 C1

Cardiff *National region capital* S Wales, UK 24 B3

Carey, Lake *Lake* Western Australia 48 B4

Caribbean Sea *Sea* W Atlantic Ocean 15 C2

Carmen SE Mexico 14 E3

Carnegie, Lake *Lake* Western Australia 48 B3

Carpentaria, Gulf of *Gulf* N Australia 49 D1

Cartagena NW Colombia 15 C3

Cartagena SE Spain 24 B6

Casablanca NW Morocco 32 B1

Caspian Sea *Inland sea* Asia/Europe 27 E4

Catania Sicily, Italy 25 E6

Catanzaro SW Italy 25 E5

Caucasus *Mountain range* Georgia/Russ. Fed. 27 D4

Cayenne *Dependent Territory capital* NE French Guiana 18 C2

Cayman Islands *UK Dependent Territory* W West Indies 15 B1

Cebu Cebu, C Philippines 45 D3

Celebes *Island* C Indonesia 45 D5

Celebes Sea *Sea* Indonesia/Philippines 45 D4

Central African Republic *Country* C Africa 33 E5

Central Siberian Plateau *Mountain range* N Russian Federation 38 C3

Ceram Sea *Sea* E Indonesia 45 E5

Ch'ongjin NE North Korea 42 D3

Chad *Country* C Africa 33 E4

Chad, Lake *Lake* C Africa 33 E5

Changchun NE China 42 D2

Changsha S China 43 B5

Chañi, Nevado de *Mountain* NW Argentina 20 C1

Channel-Port aux Basques Newfoundland, Newfoundland and Labrador, SE Canada 13 E2

Chapan, Gora *Mountain* E Turkmenistan 27 F5

Chardzhev E Turkmenistan 40 A1

Charleville Queensland, E Australia 49 E3

Charlotte North Carolina, USA 12 B4

Chattahoochee River *River* SE USA 12 A5

Cheboygan Michigan, USA 12 A2

Chech, Erg *Desert* Algeria/Mali 32 B3

Chelyabinsk C Russ. Fed. 27 F2

Chengdu C China 43 A4

Cherepovets NW Russ. Fed. 26 C1

Chernivtsi W Ukraine 26 A3

Cherskogo, Khrebet *Mountain range* NE Russian Federation 3 C1

Cheyenne Wyoming, USA 11 D3

Chiang Mai NW Thailand 44 A1

Chicago Illinois, USA 11 F3

Chico *River* S Argentina 21 B5

Chico *River* SE Argentina 21 B6

Chicoutimi Québec, SE Canada 12 C2

Chifeng N China 42 C3

Chihuahua NW Mexico 14 C1

Chile *Country* SW South America 21 B4

Chillán C Chile 20 B3

Chiloé, Isla de *Island* W Chile 21 A4

China *Country* E Asia 37 D4

Chisinau *Country capital* C Moldavia 26 A3

Chita S Russ. Fed. 42 B1

Chittagong SE Bangladesh 40 E3

Chlef NW Algeria 32 C1

Chongqing C China 43 A5

Chonos, Archipiélago de los *Island group* S Chile 21 A4

Choybalsan E Mongolia 42 B2

Christchurch South Island, NZ 51 B3

Chubut, Río *River* SE Argentina 21 B4

Chukchi Plain *Undersea feature* Arctic Ocean 52 B3

Chukchi Plateau *Undersea feature* Arctic Ocean 52 B3

Chukchi Sea *Sea* Arctic Ocean 52 B2

Chulym *River* C Russ. Fed. 38 C4

Cienfuegos C Cuba 15 C1

Cincinnati Ohio, USA 12 A4

Ciudad Bolívar E Venezuela 18 B1

Ciudad del Este SE Paraguay 20 D1

Ciudad Guayana NE Venezuela 18 B1

Ciudad Juárez N Mexico 14 C1

Ciudad Obregón NW Mexico 14 B1

Cleveland Ohio, USA 12 B3

Cloncurry Queensland, C Australia 49 D2

Cloud Peak *Mountain* Wyoming, USA 11 D3

Coats Land *Physical region* Antarctica 53 C3

Cochabamba C Bolivia 18 A5

Cochin SW India 41 C5

Cochrane Ontario, S Canada 12 B1

Coffs Harbour NSW, SE Australia 49 F4

Coimbatore S India 41 C5

Collie Western Australia 48 A4

Cologne W Germany 25 D3

Colombia *Country* N South America 18 A2

Colombo *Country capital* W Sri Lanka 41 D6

Colorado River *River* Texas, USA 10 C5

Colorado *River* Mexico/USA 8 C6

Colorado Springs Colorado, USA 11 D4

Colorado *State* C USA 11 D4

Colorado, Río *River* E Argentina 20 B3

Columbia River *River* Canada/USA 10 B2

Columbia South Carolina, USA 12 B5

Columbus Ohio, USA 12 A3

Communism Peak *Mountain* E Tajikistan 40 B2

Comodoro Rivadavia SE Argentina 21 C4

Comoros *Country* W Indian Ocean 31 E3

Conakry *Country capital* SW Guinea 32 A4

Concepción C Chile 20 B3

Concordia E Argentina 20 D2

Congo (Zaire) *Country* C Africa 30 C1

Congo Basin *Drainage basin* W Congo (Zaire) 3 A2

Congo *Country* C Africa 28 C4

Congo *River* C Africa 30 B1

Connecticut *State* NE USA 12 C3

Constanta SE Romania 26 B4

Constantine NE Algeria 33 D1

Cook Islands *Country* SW Pacific Ocean 47 E3

Cook, Mount *Mountain* NZ 51 B3

Coolgardie Western Australia 48 B4

Copenhagen *Country capital* E Denmark 25 D2

Coral Sea Islands *Australian external territory* SW Pacific Ocean 49 F2

Coral Sea *Sea* SW Pacific Ocean 49 F1

Corcovado, Golfo *Gulf* S Chile 21 A4

Córdoba C Argentina 20 C2

Cordova SW Spain 24 B6

Cork S Ireland 24 A3

Corpus Christi Texas, USA 14 D1

Corrientes NE Argentina 20 D1

Corsica *Island* France, C Mediterranean Sea 25 D5

Çorum N Turkey 26 C5

Cosenza SW Italy 25 E5

Costa Rica *Country* Central America 15 B3

Cowan, Lake *Lake* Western Australia 48 B4

Crete *Island* Greece, Aegean Sea 26 A6

Croatia *Country* SE Europe 25 E4

Croker Island *Island* Northern Territory, N Australia 48 C1

Cuba *Country* W West Indies 15 C1

Cuiabá SW Brazil 18 C5

Culiacán C Mexico 14 C2

Cumaná NE Venezuela 18 B1

Curitiba S Brazil 20 E1

Cusco C Peru 18 A5

Cyprus *Country* E Mediterranean Sea 26 B6

Czech Republic *Country* C Europe 25 D3

D

Da Lat S Vietnam 44 B3

Da Nang C Vietnam 44 B2

Dagupan N Philippines 45 D2

Dakar *Country capital* W Senegal 32 A4

Dalian NE China 42 C3

Dallas Texas, USA 11 E5

Damascus *Country capital* SW Syria 34 C1

Dandong NE China 42 C3

Daneborg N Greenland 52 B5

Danube *River* C Europe 3 A1

Dar es Salaam E Tanzania 31 E2

Darhan N Mongolia 42 A1

Darien, Gulf of *Gulf* S Caribbean Sea 15 C3

Darling River *River* NSW, SE Australia 49 D4

Darnley, Cape *Headland* Antarctica 53 B5

Darwin *Territory capital* Northern Territory, N Australia 48 C1

Dashkhovuz N Turkmenistan 27 F5

Datong C China 42 B3

Davangere W India 41 C5

Davao S Philippines 45 E3

Davis Sea *Sea* Antarctica 53 B5

Davis Strait *Strait* Baffin Bay/Labrador Sea 9 E3

Daytona Beach Florida, USA 12 B5

Death Valley *Valley* California, USA 10 B4

Deccan *Plateau* C India 41 C4

Delaware *State* NE USA 12 C4

Delhi N India 40 C3

Denmark *Country* N Europe 25 D1

Denmark Strait *Strait* Greenland/Iceland 52 A5

Denver Colorado, USA 11 D4

Des Moines Iowa, USA 11 E3

Deseado, Río *River* S Argentina 21 B5

Detroit Michigan, USA 12 A3

Devonport Tasmania, SE Australia 49 E6

Dezful SW Iran 34 E1

Dhaka *Country capital* C Bangladesh 40 E3

Dhanbad NE India 40 D3

Dibrugarh NE India 40 E3

Dijon C France 24 C4

Dili C Indonesia 45 E6

Dire Dawa E Ethiopia 35 D5

Divinópolis SE Brazil 19 D6

Djibouti *Country capital* E Djibouti 35 D4

Djibouti *Country* E Africa 35 C4

Dnipropetrovs'k E Ukraine 26 C3

Dobrich NE Bulgaria 26 B4

Dodoma *Country capital* C Tanzania 31 D2

Doha *Country capital* C Qatar 34 E2

Dominica *Country* E West Indies 15 E2

Dominican Republic *Country* C West Indies 15 D1

Don *River* SW Russ. Fed. 27 D3

Donets'k E Ukraine 26 C4

Dortmund W Germany 25 D3

Douala W Cameroon 33 D6

Drake Passage *Passage* Atlantic Ocean/Pacific Ocean 21 B6

Drakensberg *Mountain range* Lesotho/South Africa 30 C6

Dresden E Germany 25 D3

Drina *River* Bosnia and Herzegovina/Yugoslavia 25 E4

Dronning Maud Land *Physical region* Antarctica 53 C4

Dryden Ontario, C Canada 11 F1

Dubai *Emirate capital* NE UAE 34 E2

Dubbo NSW, SE Australia 49 E4

Dublin *Country capital* E Ireland 24 B2

Duluth Minnesota, USA 11 E2

Dundee E Scotland, UK 24 B2

Dunedin South Island, NZ 51 E3

Durango W Mexico 14 C2

Durban E South Africa 31 D6

Dushanbe *Country capital* W Tajikistan 40 B1

E

East China Sea *Sea* W Pacific Ocean 43 C5

East Indies *Island group* SE Asia 3 C2

East London S South Africa 31 D6

East Novaya Zemlya Trough *Undersea feature* W Kara Sea 52 C4

East Siberian Sea *Sea* Arctic Ocean 39 D2

Edinburgh *National region capital* S Scotland, UK 24 B2

Edmonton Alberta, SW Canada 10 C1

Éfaté *Island* C Vanuatu 50 D3

Egypt *Country* NE Africa 34 B3

El Giza N Egypt 34 B2

El Minya C Egypt 34 B2

El Obeid C Sudan 35 B4

El Paso Texas, USA 11 D5

El Salvador *Country* Central America 15 A3

Elbert, Mount *Mountain* Colorado, USA 11 D4

Elblåg N Poland 25 E2

Ellesmere Island *Island* Queen Elizabeth Islands, NW Terr., N Canada 9 D2

Ellsworth Land *Physical region* Antarctica 53 B2

Emi Koussi *Mountain* N Chad 33 E3

Emory Peak *Mountain* Texas, USA 14 C1

Enderby Land *Physical region* Antarctica 53 C5

English Channel *Channel* NW Europe 24 C3

Épi *Island* C Vanuatu 50 D3

Equatorial Guinea *Country* C Africa 33 D6

Erdenet N Mongolia 42 A1

Erebus, Mount *Volcano* Ross Island, Antarctica 53 A4

Erie Pennsylvania, USA 12 B3

Erie, Lake *Lake* Canada/USA 12 B3

Eritrea *Country* E Africa 35 C4

Esperance Western Australia 48 B5

Espiritu Santo *Island* W Vanuatu 50 D3

Estados, Isla de los *Island* S Argentina 21 C6

Estonia *Country* NE Europe 26 A1

Ethiopia *Country* E Africa 35 C5

Ethiopian Highlands *Plateau* N Ethiopia 35 C5

Etna, Mount *Volcano* Sicily, Italy, C Mediterranean Sea 25 E6

Eugene Oregon, USA 10 A3

Europe *Continent* 3 A1

Everest, Mount *Mountain* China/Nepal 40 D3

Exmouth Western Australia 48 A3

F

Faisalabad NE Pakistan 40 B2

Falkland Islands *UK Dependent Territory* SW Atlantic Ocean 21 D5

Fargo North Dakota, USA 11 E2

Feira de Santana E Brazil 19 E5

Fez N Morocco 32 C1

Fianarantsoa C Madagascar 31 F4

Fiji *Country* SW Pacific Ocean 50 E3

Finland *Country* N Europe 38 A2

Florence C Italy 25 D4

Flores Sea *Sea* C Indonesia 43 D6

Florianópolis S Brazil 20 E1

Florida *State* SE USA 12 A6

Florida, Straits of *Strait* Atlantic Ocean/Gulf of Mexico 15 C1

Fongafale *Country capital* Funafuti Atoll, SE Tuvalu 50 F2

Fort Albany Ontario, C Canada 12 B1

Fort Lauderdale Florida, USA 12 B6

Fortaleza NE Brazil 19 E3

Foxe Basin *Sea* NW Terr., N Canada 9 D3

Fram Basin *Undersea feature* Arctic Ocean 52 B4

France *Country* W Europe 24 C4

Frankfurt am Main SW Germany 25 D3

Franz Josef Land *Island group* Russ. Fed. 38 C2

Freetown *Country capital* W Sierra Leone 32 A5

Fremantle Western Australia 48 A4

French Guiana *French Dependent Territory* N South America 18 C2

French Polynesia *Country* SW Pacific Ocean 47 E4

Fresnillo C Mexico 14 C2

Fresno California, USA 10 B4

Fukuoka SW Japan 43 D4

Fukushima C Japan 42 F3

Funafuti *Island group* N Vanuatu 47 D3

Fuxin NE China 42 C3

Fuzhou SE China 43 C5

G

Gabon *Country* C Africa 30 A1

Gaborone *Country capital* SE Botswana 30 C5

Gairdner, Lake *Salt lake* South Australia 49 D4

Galán, Cerro *Mountain* NW Argentina 20 B1

Galapagos Islands *Island group* Ecuador 3 E2

Gambia *Country* W Africa 32 A4

Ganca N Azerbaijan 27 D5

Gander Newfoundland, Newfoundland and Labrador, SE Canada 13 E2

Ganges *River* Bangladesh/India 40 D2

Ganges, Mouths of the *Delta* Bangladesh/India 41 E4

Ganzhou S China 43 B5

Garoua N Cameroon 33 E5

Gaziantep S Turkey 26 C6

Gdynia N Poland 25 E2

Geelong Victoria, SE Australia 49 E5

Gejiu S China 44 B1

General Santos S Philippines 45 D3

Geneva SW Switzerland 24 C4

Genoa NW Italy 25 D4

George Town Peninsular Malaysia 44 A4

George V Land *Physical region* Antarctica 53 B4

Georgetown *Country capital* N Guyana 18 D2

Georgia *Country* SW Asia 27 D5

Georgia *State* SE USA 12 A5

Geraldton Western Australia 48 A4

Germany *Country* N Europe 25 D3

Ghana *Country* W Africa 32 C5

Gibraltar *UK Dependent Territory* SW Europe 24 B6

Gibraltar, Strait of *Strait* Atlantic Ocean/ Mediterranean Sea 24 A6

Gibson Desert *Desert* Western Australia 48 B3

Gijón N Spain 24 B4

Glacier Peak *Mountain* Washington, USA 10 B2

Gladstone Queensland, E Australia 49 E3

Glasgow C Scotland, UK 24 B2

Glazov NW Russ. Fed. 27 E1

Gobi *Desert* China/Mongolia 42 A3

Godoy Cruz W Argentina 20 B2

Goiânia C Brazil 19 D5

Good Hope, Cape of *Headland* SW South Africa 30 B6

Gorakhpur N India 40 D3

Gorgan N Iran 27 E6

Gothenburg S Sweden 25 D1

Goulburn NSW, SE Australia 49 E5

Governador Valadares SE Brazil 19 D6

Grafton NSW, SE Australia 49 F4

Granada S Spain 24 B6

Grand Banks of Newfoundland *Undersea feature* NW Atlantic Ocean 13 E2

Grand Canyon *Canyon* Arizona, USA 10 C4

Grand Erg Occidental *Desert* W Algeria 32 C2

Grande, Bahía *Bay* S Argentina 21 B5

Grande, Rio *River* Mexico/USA 11 E6

Great Australian Bight *Bight* S Australia 48 C4

Great Barrier Reef *Reef* Queensland, NE Australia 49 E2

Great Bear Lake *Lake* NW Terr., NW Canada 8 C3

Great Dividing Range *Mountain range* NE Australia 49 E3

Great Falls Montana, USA 10 C2

Great Karoo *Plateau region* S South Africa 30 C6

Great Lakes *Lakes* Canada/USA 3 E2

Great Rift Valley *Depression* Asia/Africa 3 B2

Great Sandy Desert *Desert* Western Australia 48 B2

Great Slave Lake *Lake* NW Terr., NW Canada 8 C4

Great Victoria Desert *Desert* South Australia/Western Australia 48 B4

Greater Antarctica *Physical region* Antarctica 53 B4

Greece *Country* SE Europe 25 E5

Green Bay Wisconsin, USA 11 F3

Greenland *Danish Dependent Territory* NE North America 9 E2

Greenland Sea *Sea* Arctic Ocean 52 B5

Grenada *Country capital* SE West Indies 15 E3

Groznyy SW Russ. Fed. 27 D4

Guadalajara C Mexico 14 C3

Guadalcanal *Island* C Solomon Islands 50 C2

Guadalupe Peak *Mountain* Texas, USA 11 D5

Guadeloupe *French Dependent Territory* E West Indies 15 E2

Guam *US Dependent Territory* W Pacific Ocean 46 A2

Guangyuan C China 43 A4

Guangzhou S China 43 B6

Guantánamo SE Cuba 15 C1

Guaporé, Rio *River* Bolivia/Brazil 18 B5

Guatemala City *Country capital* C Guatemala 15 A2

Guatemala *Country* Central America 15 B2

Guiana Highlands *Mountain range* N South America 18 B2

Guilin S China 43 B5

Guinea *Country* W Africa 32 A5

Guinea, Gulf of *Gulf* E Atlantic Ocean 3 A2

Guinea-Bissau *Country* W Africa 32 A5

Guiyang S China 43 A5

Gujranwala NE Pakistan 40 C2

Gulf, The *Gulf* SW Asia 34 E2

Gunnbjørn Fjeld *Mountain* C Greenland 52 A5

Gusau N Nigeria 33 D5
Guwahati NE India 40 E3
Guyana *Country* N South America 18 B2
Gwalior C India 40 C3
Gympie Queensland, E Australia 49 F3

H

Hachinohe C Japan 42 F3
Hai Phong N Vietnam 44 B1
Haicheng NE China 42 C3
Haikou S China 44 C1
Hainan *Province* S China 44 C1
Haiti *Country* C West Indies 15 D2
Hakodate NE Japan 42 F3
Halifax Nova Scotia, SE Canada 13 D2
Hamah W Syria 34 C1
Hamamatsu S Japan 43 E4
Hamburg N Germany 25 D2
Hamersley Range *Mountain range* Western Australia 48 A3
Hamhung N North Korea 42 D3
Hamilton *Dependent Territory capital* C Bermuda 13 D5
Hamilton North Island, NZ 51 F2
Hamilton Ontario, S Canada 12 B3
Hangzhou SE China 43 C5
Hanoi *Country capital* N Vietnam 44 B1
Hanzhong C China 43 A4
Harare *Country capital* NE Zimbabwe 31 D3
Harbin NE China 42 D2
Hargeysa NW Somalia 35 D5
Hartford Connecticut, USA 9 E5
Hastings North Island, NZ 51 F2
Havana *Country capital* W Cuba 15 B1
Havre-St-Pierre Québec, E Canada 13 D1
Hawaiian Islands *Island group* Hawaii, USA, C Pacific Ocean 3 D2
Hearst Ontario, S Canada 12 A1
Hefei E China 43 C4
Hegang NE China 42 D2
Helsingborg S Sweden 25 D2
Helsinki *Country capital* S Finland 38 A2
Hengyang S China 43 B5
Henzada SW Burma 41 F4
Herat W Afghanistan 40 A2
Hermosillo NW Mexico 14 B1
Himalayas *Mountain range* S Asia 40 D2
Hindu Kush *Mountain range* Afghanistan/Pakistan 3 B2
Hirosaki C Japan 42 F3
Hiroshima SW Japan 43 E4
Hitachi S Japan 43 F4

Hkakabo Razi *Mountain* Burma/China 40 F2
Hô Chi Minh S Vietnam 44 B3
Hobart Tasmania, SE Australia 49 E6
Hohhot N China 42 B3
Homyel' SE Belorussia 26 B2
Honduras *Country* Central America 15 B2
Hong Kong S China 43 B6
Honiara *Country capital* C Solomon Islands 50 C2
Honshu *Island* SW Japan 42 F3
Horn, Cape *Headland* S Chile 3 E3
Houston Texas, USA 11 E5
Hovsgol, Lake *Lake* N Mongolia 42 A1
Hrodna W Belorussia 25 F2
Huaihua S China 43 B5
Huainan E China 43 B4
Huambo C Angola 30 B3
Hubli SW India 41 C5
Hudson Bay *Bay* NE Canada 9 D4
Hudson Strait *Strait* NW Terr./Québec, NE Canada 9 E4
Hue C Vietnam 44 B2
Huelva SW Spain 24 B6
Hulun Nur *Lake* NE China 42 C1
Humboldt River *River* Nevada, USA 10 B3
Hungary *Country* C Europe 25 E4
Hunter Island *Island* Tasmania, SE Australia 49 E6
Huron, Lake *Lake* Canada/USA 12 A2
Hyderabad C India 41 C4
Hyderabad SE Pakistan 40 B3

I

Ibadan SW Nigeria 33 D5
Iberia *Physical region* Portugal/Spain 3 A2
Iceland *Country* N Atlantic Ocean 9 F2
Iceland Plateau *Undersea feature* S Greenland Sea 52 B6
Idaho *State* NW USA 10 B3
Iguidi, 'Erg *Desert* Algeria/Mauritania 32 B2
Ilebo W Congo (Zaire) 30 C1
Iligan S Philippines 45 D3
Illinois *State* C USA 11 F3
Iloilo C Philippines 45 D3
Imperatriz NE Brazil 19 D4
Imphal NE India 40 E3
India *Country* S Asia 41 C4
Indian Ocean *Ocean* 3 B2
Indiana *State* N USA 12 A3
Indianapolis Indiana, USA 12 A3

Indigirka *River* NE Russian Federation 39 E2
Indonesia *Country* SE Asia 44 C5
Indore C India 40 C3
Indus *River* S Asia 40 B2
Indus, Mouths of the *Delta* S Pakistan 40 B3
Inhambane SE Mozambique 31 D5
Inner Mongolia *Autonomous region* N China 39 E5
Inuvik NW Terr., NW Canada 52 A2
Invercargill South Island, NZ 51 E3
Inyangani *Mountain* NE Zimbabwe 31 D4
Iowa *State* C USA 11 F3
Ipoh Peninsular Malaysia 44 B4
Ipswich Queensland, E Australia 49 F4
Iquique N Chile 18 A6
Iquitos N Peru 18 A3
Irakleio Crete, Greece 26 A6
Iran *Country* SW Asia 34 E1
Iranian Plateau *Plateau* N Iran 34 E1
Iraq *Country* SW Asia 34 D1
Irbid N Jordan 34 C1
Ireland, Republic of *Country* NW Europe 24 A2
Irian Jaya *Province* E Indonesia 45 F5
Irkutsk S Russ. Fed. 42 A1
Irrawaddy *River* W Burma 44 A1
Isfahan C Iran 34 E1
Islamabad *Country capital* NE Pakistan 40 C2
Israel *Country* SW Asia 34 C1
Istanbul NW Turkey 26 B5
Itabuna E Brazil 19 E5
Itaipú, Represa de *Reservoir* Brazil/Paraguay 20 D1
Italy *Country* S Europe 25 D5
Ivory Coast *Country* W Africa 32 B5
Iwaki N Japan 42 F3
Izhevsk NW Russ. Fed. 27 E1
Izmir W Turkey 26 B5

J

Jabalpur C India 40 D3
Jackson Mississippi, USA 11 F5
Jacksonville Florida, USA 12 B5
Jaffna N Sri Lanka 41 D5
Jaipur N India 40 C3
Jakarta *Country capital* Java, C Indonesia 44 B5
Jalalabad E Afghanistan 40 B2
Jamaica *Country* W West Indies 15 C2
Jambi Sumatra, W Indonesia 44 B5
James Bay *Bay* Ontario/Québec, E Canada 12 B1

Jamshedpur NE India 40 D3

Jan Mayen *Norwegian Dependent Territory* N Atlantic Ocean 52 B5

Japan *Country* E Asia 42 E3

Japan, Sea of *Sea* NW Pacific Ocean 42 E3

Japurá, Rio *River* Brazil/Colombia 18 A3

Jarvis Island *Dependent Territory* C Pacific Ocean 47 E3

Java *Island* C Indonesia 44 B6

Java Sea *Sea* W Indonesia 44 B5

Javari, Rio *River* Brazil/Peru 18 A3

Jayapura E Indonesia 45 F5

Jaz Murian, Hamun-e *Lake* SE Iran 34 F2

Jedda W Saudi Arabia 34 C3

Jember Java, C Indonesia 44 C6

Jérémie SW Haiti 15 D2

Jerusalem *Country capital* NE Israel 34 C1

Jiangmen S China 43 B6

Jilin NE China 42 D2

Jinan E China 43 C4

Jingdezhen S China 43 B5

Jinhua SE China 43 C5

Jinzhou NE China 42 C3

Jixi NE China 42 D2

João Pessoa E Brazil 19 E4

Jodhpur NW India 40 C3

Johannesburg NE South Africa 30 C5

Joinville S Brazil 20 E1

Jönköping S Sweden 25 E1

Jordan *Country* SW Asia 34 C2

Joseph Bonaparte Gulf *Gulf* N Australia 48 C1

Juazeiro do Norte E Brazil 19 E4

Juazeiro E Brazil 19 E4

Juba *River* Ethiopia/Somalia 35 D6

Juba S Sudan 35 B5

Juruá, Rio *River* Brazil/Peru 18 A4

Juruena, Rio *River* W Brazil 18 B5

K

K2 *Mountain* China/Pakistan 40 C1

Kabul *Country capital* E Afghanistan 40 B2

Kabwe C Zambia 31 D3

Kaduna C Nigeria 33 D5

Kagoshima SW Japan 43 D4

Kaifeng C China 43 B4

Kalahari Desert *Desert* Southern Africa 30 C4

Kalbarri Western Australia 48 A4

Kalemie SE Congo (Zaire) 31 D2

Kalgoorlie Western Australia 48 B4

Kalimantan *Geopolitical region* C Indonesia 44 C5

Kalyan W India 41 C4

Kamchatka *River* E Russian Federation 39 F2

Kamina S Congo (Zaire) 30 C2

Kamloops British Columbia, SW Canada 10 B1

Kampala *Country capital* S Uganda 35 B6

Kananga S Congo (Zaire) 30 C2

Kandahar S Afghanistan 40 B2

Kandy C Sri Lanka 41 D6

Kangaroo Island *Island* South Australia 49 D5

Kano N Nigeria 33 D5

Kanpur N India 40 D3

Kansas City Kansas, USA 11 E4

Kansas City Missouri, USA 11 E4

Kansas *State* C USA 11 D4

Kaohsiung S Taiwan 43 C6

Kaolack W Senegal 32 A4

Kara Sea *Sea* Arctic Ocean 38 B3

Karachi SE Pakistan 40 B3

Karaganda C Kazakhstan 38 B5

Karakol N Kyrgyzstan 38 B5

Kariba, Lake *Reservoir* Zambia/Zimbabwe 30 C3

Kashan C Iran 34 E1

Kassala E Sudan 35 C4

Katahdin, Mount *Mountain* Maine, USA 12 C2

Katanning Western Australia 48 A5

Katherine Northern Territory, N Australia 48 C1

Kathmandu *Country capital* C Nepal 40 D3

Katsina N Nigeria 33 D5

Kaunas C Lithuania 25 F2

Kavir, Dasht-e *Salt pan* N Iran 34 E1

Kazakhstan *Country* C Asia 27 E3

Kazan' W Russ. Fed. 27 E2

Kelowna British Columbia, SW Canada 10 B1

Kemp Land *Physical region* Antarctica 53 C5

Kentucky *State* C USA 12 A4

Kenya *Country* E Africa 35 C6

Kerch SE Ukraine 26 C4

Kerguelen *Island* C French Southern and Antarctic Territories 3 B3

Kerman C Iran 34 F2

Khabarovsk SE Russ. Fed. 42 E2

Khambhat, Gulf of *Gulf* W India 41 C4

Khanka, Lake *Lake* China/Russ. Fed. 42 E2

Kharkiv NE Ukraine 26 C3

Khartoum *Country capital* C Sudan 35 B4

Kherson S Ukraine 26 B4

Kheta *River* N. Russ. Fed. 39 D3

Khouribga C Morocco 32 B1

Khulna SW Bangladesh 40 E3

Khvoy NW Iran 27 D5

Kiel N Germany 25 D2

Kielce SE Poland 25 E3

Kiev *Country capital* N Ukraine 26 B3

Kigali *Country capital* C Rwanda 31 D1

Kikwit W Congo (Zaire) 30 B1

Kilimanjaro *Volcano* NE Tanzania 31 E1

Kimberley C South Africa 30 C5

Kimberley Plateau *Plateau* Western Australia 48 B2

Kimch'aek E North Korea 42 D3

Kineshma W Russ. Fed. 27 D1

King Island *Island* Tasmania, SE Australia 49 E6

Kingman Arizona, USA 10 C4

Kingman Reef *Dependent Territory* C Pacific Ocean 47 D2

Kingston *Country capital* E Jamaica 15 C2

Kinshasa *Country capital* W Congo (Zaire) 30 B1

Kinyeti *Mountain* S Sudan 35 B6

Kiribati *Country* C Pacific Ocean 47 D3

Kirinyaga *Volcano* C Kenya 35 C5

Kirkpatrick, Mount *Mountain* Antarctica 53 A4

Kirkuk N Iraq 34 D1

Kirov NW Russ. Fed. 27 E1

Kisangani NE Congo (Zaire) 35 A6

Kismaayo S Somalia 35 D6

Kisumu W Kenya 35 C6

Kitakyushu SW Japan 43 D4

Kitami NE Japan 42 F2

Kitwe C Zambia 30 C3

Klaipėda NW Lithuania 25 F2

Knud Rasmussen Land *Physical region* N Greenland 52 A4

Kobe SW Japan 43 E4

Kochi Shikoku, SW Japan 43 E4

Kola Peninsula *Peninsula* NW Russ. Fed. 52 C5

Kolhapur SW India 41 C4

Kolyma Range *Mountain range* E Russ. Fed. 39 E2

Kolyma *River* NE Russ. Fed. 39 E2

Komsomol'sk-na-Amure SE Russ. Fed. 42 E1

Kong Frederik VIII Land *Physical region* NE Greenland 52 A5

Konya C Turkey 26 B6

Korea Bay *Bay* China/North Korea 42 C3

Korea Strait Japan/South Korea 43 D4

Koszalin NW Poland 25 E2

Kota Bharu Peninsular Malaysia 44 B3

Madrid Country capital C Spain 24 B5

Madurai S India 41 D5

Maewo Island C Vanuatu 50 D3

Magadan E Russ. Fed. 39 E3

Magellan, Strait of Strait Argentina/Chile 21 B6

Magnitogorsk C Russ. Fed. 27 F2

Mahajanga NW Madagascar 31 F3

Mahalapye SE Botswana 30 C4

Mahilyow E Belorussia 26 B2

Maiduguri NE Nigeria 33 E5

Maine State NE USA 12 C3

Maine, Gulf of Gulf NE USA 13 D3

Majuro Country capital Tarawa, NW Kiribati 46 C2

Makarov Basin Undersea feature Arctic Ocean 52 B4

Makhachkala SW Russ. Fed. 27 D4

Makurdi C Nigeria 33 D5

Malabo Country capital Isla de Bioco, NW Equatorial Guinea 33 D6

Málaga S Spain 24 B6

Malaita Island N Solomon Islands 50 C2

Malang Java, C Indonesia 44 C6

Malatya SE Turkey 26 C5

Malawi Country S Africa 31 D2

Malay Peninsula Peninsula Malaysia/Thailand 44 A3

Malaysia Country SE Asia 44 B4

Maldives Country N Indian Ocean 41 C6

Male' Country capital C Maldives 41 C6

Malekula Island W Vanuatu 50 D3

Mali Country W Africa 32 C4

Malmö S Sweden 25 D2

Malta Country C Mediterranean Sea 25 E6

Mamoré, Rio River Bolivia/Brazil 18 B5

Manado Celebes, C Indonesia 45 D4

Managua Country capital W Nicaragua 15 B3

Manama Country capital N Bahrain 34 E2

Manaus NW Brazil 18 B3

Manchester NW England, UK 24 B2

Manchurian Plain Plain NE China 3 C2

Mandalay C Burma 44 A1

Mandurah Western Australia 48 A5

Mangalore W India 41 C5

Manila Country capital N Philippines 45 D2

Manitoba Province S Canada 9 D5

Manitoba, Lake Lake Manitoba, S Canada 11 D1

Manurewa North Island, NZ 51 F2

Manzanillo SW Mexico 14 C3

Manzhouli N China 42 C1

Maoming S China 43 B6

Maputo Country capital S Mozambique 31 D5

Mar Chiquita, Laguna Lake C Argentina 20 C2

Mar del Plata E Argentina 20 D3

Maracaibo NW Venezuela 18 A1

Maradi S Niger 33 D4

Marajó, Baía de Bay N Brazil 19 D3

Marajó, Ilha de Island N Brazil 18 C3

Marble Bar Western Australia 48 B2

Marie Byrd Land Physical region Antarctica 53 B3

Marília S Brazil 20 E1

Maringá S Brazil 20 D1

Marka S Somalia 35 D6

Markham, Mount Mountain Antarctica 53 A4

Maroua N Cameroon 33 E5

Marrakech W Morocco 32 B1

Marseille SE France 24 C4

Marshall Islands Country W Pacific Ocean 46 C2

Martinique French Dependent Territory E West Indies 15 E2

Maryborough Queensland, E Australia 49 F3

Maryland State NE USA 12 C4

Maseru Country capital W Lesotho 30 C5

Mashhad NE Iran 34 F1

Massachusetts State NE USA 12 C3

Matadi W Congo (Zaire) 30 B2

Matanzas NW Cuba 15 C1

Mataram C Indonesia 44 C6

Mato Grosso Region W Brazil 3 F3

Matsue SW Japan 43 E4

Matsumoto S Japan 43 E4

Maturín NE Venezuela 18 B1

Mauritania Country W Africa 32 A4

Mauritius Island N Indian Ocean 3 B3

Mayotte French Dependent Territory, E Africa 31 E3

Mazatlán C Mexico 14 C2

Mbabane Country capital NW Swaziland 31 D5

Mbandaka NW Congo (Zaire) 30 B1

Mbuji-Mayi S Congo (Zaire) 30 C2

Mckinley, Mount Mountain Alaska, USA 8 B3

Mecca W Saudi Arabia 34 C3

Medan Sumatra, E Indonesia 44 A4

Medina C Saudi Arabia 34 C2

Mediterranean Sea Sea Africa/Asia/Europe 3 A2

Meerut N India 40 C2

Meiktila C Burma 44 A1

Mekong River SE Asia 44 B2

Melanesia Island group W Pacific Ocean 50 D2

Melbourne Victoria, SE Australia 49 E5

Melitopol' SE Ukraine 26 C4

Melliza Sur, Cerro Mountain S Chile 21 B5

Melville Island Island Northern Territory, N Australia 48 C1

Memphis Tennessee, USA 11 F4

Mendeleyev Ridge Undersea feature Arctic Ocean 52 B3

Mendoza W Argentina 20 B2

Mérida SW Mexico 14 E2

Mérida W Venezuela 18 A1

Mesa Arizona, USA 10 C5

Messina Sicily, Italy 25 E6

Meta, Río River Colombia/ Venezuela 18 A2

Mexicali NW Mexico 14 B1

Mexico City Country capital C Mexico 14 D3

Mexico Country N Central America 14 C2

Mexico, Gulf of Gulf W Atlantic Ocean 3 E2

Miami Florida, USA 12 B6

Mianyang C China 43 A4

Michigan State N USA 12 A2

Michigan, Lake Lake N USA 12 A2

Micronesia Country W Pacific Ocean 46 B2

Middlesbrough N England, UK 24 B2

Milan N Italy 25 D4

Mildura Victoria, SE Australia 49 D5

Milwaukee Wisconsin, USA 11 F3

Mindanao Island S Philippines 45 E3

Minneapolis Minnesota, USA 11 E2

Minnesota State N USA 11 E2

Minsk Country capital C Belorussia 26 B2

Mirim Lagoon Lagoon Brazil/Uruguay 20 D2

Misratah NW Libya 33 E1

Mississippi River River Ontario, SE Canada 3 E2

Mississippi River USA 11 F5

Mississippi State SE USA 11 F5

Missouri River River C USA 11 F3

Missouri State C USA 11 E4

Mitchell, Mount Mountain North Carolina, USA 12 B4

Miyazaki SW Japan 43 D4

Mobile Alabama, USA 9 D6

Môco *Mountain* W Angola 30 B3

Modesto California, USA 10 B4

Mogadishu *Country capital* S Somalia 35 D6

Moldavia *Country* SE Europe 26 A4

Mombasa SE Kenya 31 E1

Monaco *Country capital* S Monaco 25 D5

Monclova NE Mexico 14 D2

Moncton New Brunswick, SE Canada 13 D2

Mongolia *Country* E Asia 39 D5

Monrovia *Country capital* W Liberia 32 B6

Montana *State* NW USA 10 C2

Monterría N Colombia 15 C3

Monterrey NE Mexico 14 D2

Montes Claros SE Brazil 19 D5

Montevideo *Country capital* S Uruguay 20 D3

Montgomery Alabama, USA 12 A5

Montréal Québec, SE Canada 12 C2

Montserrat *UK Dependent Territory* E West Indies 15 D2

Moore, Lake *Lake* Western Australia 48 A4

Moosonee Ontario, SE Canada 12 B1

Moree NSW, SE Australia 49 E4

Morelia S Mexico 14 C3

Morocco *Country* N Africa 32 B1

Moroni *Country capital* Grande Comore, NW Comoros 31 E3

Morris Jesup, Kap *Headland* N Greenland 52 B4

Moscow *Country capital* W Russ. Fed. 26 C2

Mossoró NE Brazil 19 E3

Mosul N Iraq 27 D6

Moulmein S Burma 44 A2

Moundou SW Chad 33 E5

Mount Gambier South Australia 49 D5

Mount Isa Queensland, C Australia 49 D2

Mount Magnet Western Australia 48 A4

Mozambique Channel *Strait* W Indian Ocean 31 E5

Mozambique *Country* S Africa 31 D4

Mudanjiang NE China 42 D2

Multan E Pakistan 40 B2

Munich SE Germany 25 D3

Murmansk NW Russ. Fed. 38 B2

Muroran NE Japan 42 F3

Musa, Gebel *Mountain* NE Egypt 34 C2

Muscat *Country capital* NE Oman 34 F3

Myingyan C Burma 44 A1

Mysore W India 41 C5

N

Naberezhnyye Chelny W Russ. Fed. 27 E2

Nadi Viti Levu, W Fiji 50 E3

Naga N Philippines 45 D2

Nagoya SW Japan 43 E4

Nagpur C India 41 C4

Nairobi *Country capital* S Kenya 31 D1

Nakhodka SE Russ. Fed. 42 E2

Nal'chik SW Russ. Fed. 27 D4

Namib Desert *Desert* W Namibia 30 B4

Namibe SW Angola 30 A3

Namibia *Country* S Africa 30 B4

Nampula NE Mozambique 31 E3

Nanchang S China 39 E6

Nanjing E China 43 C4

Nanning S China 43 A6

Nanping SE China 43 C5

Nansen Basin *Undersea feature* Arctic Ocean 52 B3

Nansen Cordillera *Undersea feature* Arctic Ocean 52 B3

Nantes NW France 24 B4

Nanyang C China 43 B4

Naples S Italy 25 E5

Nares Strait *Strait* Canada/ Greenland 52 B4

Nashik W India 41 C4

Nashville Tennessee, USA 12 A4

Nassau *Country capital* New Providence, N Bahamas 15 C1

Nasser, Lake *Lake* Egypt/Sudan 34 B3

Natal E Brazil 19 E4

Natitingou NW Benin 32 C5

Nauru *Country* W Pacific Ocean 50 D1

Navapolatsk N Belorussia 26 B2

Navassa Island *US Dependent Territory* C West Indies 15 C2

Nawabshah S Pakistan 40 B3

Ndjamena *Country capital* W Chad 33 E5

Ndola C Zambia 31 D3

Neblina, Pico da *Mountain* NW Brazil 18 A3

Nebraska *State* C USA 11 D3

Negro, Río *River* Brazil/Uruguay 20 D2

Negro, Rio *River* N South America 18 B3

Nellore E India 41 C5

Nelson South Island, NZ 51 E2

Nepal *Country* S Asia 40 D3

Netherlands *Country* NW Europe 24 C2

Netherlands Antilles *Dutch autonomous region* S Caribbean Sea 15 D3

Nevada *State* W USA 10 B4

New Britain *Island* E PNG 50 B2

New Brunswick *Province* SE Canada 13 D2

New Caledonia *French Dependent Territory*, SW Pacific Ocean 46 C4

New Delhi *Country capital* N India 40 C3

New Georgia Islands *Island group* NW Solomon Islands 50 B2

New Guinea *Island* Indonesia/PNG 45 F5

New Hampshire *State* NE USA 12 C3

New Ireland *Island* NE PNG 50 B1

New Jersey *State* NE USA 12 C3

New Mexico *State* SW USA 11 D5

New Orleans Louisiana, USA 11 F6

New Plymouth North Island, NZ 51 E2

New Siberian Islands *Island group* N Russ. Fed. 52 C3

New South Wales *State* SE Australia 49 E4

New York New York, USA 12 C3

New York *State* NE USA 12 B3

New Zealand *Country* SW Pacific Ocean 51 E2

Newcastle NSW, SE Australia 49 F4

Newfoundland and Labrador *Province*, E Canada 9 E4

Newfoundland *Island* Newfoundland and Labrador, SE Canada 13 F2

Neyveli SE India 41 D5

Nha Trang S Vietnam 44 C3

Niamey *Country capital* SW Niger 32 C4

Nicaragua *Country* Central America 15 B3

Nicobar Islands *Island group* India, E Indian Ocean 41 E6

Nicosia *Country capital* C Cyprus 36 B6

Niger *Country* W Africa 33 D4

Niger *River* W Africa 32 C4

Nigeria *Country* W Africa 33 D5

Niigata C Japan 42 E3

Nile *River* N Africa 34 B2

Niue *Country* SW Pacific Ocean 47 D4

Nizhniy Novgorod W Russ. Fed. 27 D2

Nobeoka SW Japan 43 D4

Nome Alaska, USA 52 A1

Norfolk Island *French Dependent Territory* SW Pacific Ocean 46 C5

Norfolk Virginia, USA 12 B4

Noril'sk N Russ. Fed. 38 C3

Norrköping S Sweden 25 E1

North America *Continent* 3 E1

North American Basin *Undersea feature* W Sargasso Sea 3 F2

North Cape *Headland* N Norway 52 C5

North Cape *Headland* North Island, NZ 51 E1

North Carolina *State* SE USA 12 B4

North Dakota *State* N USA 11 D2

North Geomagnetic Pole *Pole* Arctic Ocean 52 A3

North Island *Island* N NZ 51 C2

North Korea *Country* E Asia 42 D3

North Pole *Pole* Arctic Ocean 52 B4

North Sea *Sea* NW Europe 24 C2

Northern Dvina *River* NW Russian Federation 38 B3

Northern Mariana Islands *US Dependent Territory* W Pacific Ocean 46 B2

Northern Territory *Territory* N Australia 48 C2

Northwest Territories *Territory* NW Canada 8 C3

Northwind Plain *Undersea feature* Arctic Ocean 52 A2

Norway *Country* N Europe 38 A2

Norwegian Sea *Sea* NE Atlantic Ocean 38 A1

Nouâdhibou W Mauritania 32 A3

Nouakchott *Country capital* SW Mauritania 32 A4

Nouméa *Dependent Territory capital* S New Caledonia 46 C4

Nova Iguaçu SE Brazil 19 D6

Nova Scotia *Province* SE Canada 13 D2

Novaya Zemlya *Island group* N Russ. Fed. 38 B2

Novgorod W Russ. Fed. 26 B1

Novi Sad N Yugoslavia 25 D3

Novokuznetsk S Russ. Fed. 38 C5

Novosibirsk C Russ. Fed. 38 C4

Novosibirskiye Ostrova *Island group* N Russian Federation 39 D2

Nubian Desert *Desert* NE Sudan 34 C3

Nuku'alofa S Tonga 47 D4

Nukus W Uzbekistan 27 F5

Nullarbor Plain *Plateau* South Australia / Western Australia 48 C4

Nuremberg S Germany 25 D3

Nyala W Sudan 35 A4

Nyasa, Lake *Lake* E Africa 31 D3

Nyeri C Kenya 35 C6

O

Oaxaca SE Mexico 14 D3

Ob' *River* C Russ. Fed. 38 B3

Ocean Falls British Columbia, SW Canada 10 A1

Odense C Denmark 25 D2

Odesa SW Ukraine 26 B4

Ogaden *Plateau* Ethiopia / Somalia 35 D5

Ogbomosho W Nigeria 33 D5

Ohio River *River* N USA 12 A4

Ohio *State* N USA 12 A3

Ojos del Salado, Cerro *Mountain* W Argentina 20 B1

Okavango Delta *Wetland* N Botswana 30 C4

Okayama SW Japan 43 E4

Okeechobee, Lake *Lake* SE USA 12 B6

Okhotsk, Sea of *Sea* NW Pacific Ocean 39 F3

Oklahoma City Oklahoma, USA 11 E4

Oklahoma *State* C USA 11 E5

Olenëk *River* NE Russ. Fed. 39 D3

Omaha Nebraska, USA 11 E3

Oman *Country* SW Asia 34 D4

Oman, Gulf of *Gulf* N Arabian Sea 34 F2

Omdurman C Sudan 35 B4

Omsk C Russ. Fed. 38 B4

Onega, Lake *Lake* NW Russian Federation 38 A3

Ongole E India 41 D5

Ontario *Province* S Canada 9 D5

Ontario, Lake *Lake* Canada / USA 12 B3

Oporto NW Portugal 24 A5

Oran N Algeria 32 C1

Orange NSW, SE Australia 49 E4

Orange River *River* S Africa 30 B5

Ordu N Turkey 26 C5

Örebro C Sweden 25 E1

Oregon *State* NW USA 10 A3

Orenburg W Russ. Fed. 27 E3

Oreor *Country capital* N Palau 45 F3

Orinoco, Río *River* Colombia / Venezuela 18 A1

Orkney Islands *Island group* N Scotland, UK 24 B1

Orlando Florida, USA 12 B6

Orléans C France 24 C4

Orsha NE Belorussia 26 B2

Orsk W Russ. Fed. 27 F3

Oruro W Bolivia 18 A5

Osh SW Kyrgyzstan 38 B5

Oshkosh Wisconsin, USA 11 F3

Oslo *Country capital* S Norway 25 D1

Ostrov Vrangelya *Island* NE Russian Federation 39 F1

Ottawa *Country capital* Ontario, SE Canada 12 B2

Ouagadougou *Country capital* C Burkina 32 C5

Oujda NE Morocco 32 C1

Ourense NW Spain 24 B5

Outer Hebrides *Island group* NW Scotland, UK 24 B1

Owen Stanley Range *Mountain range* S PNG 50 A2

Owen, Mount *Mountain* South Island, NZ 51 E2

Oxford S England, UK 24 B3

P

Pacific Ocean *Ocean* 3 D2

Padang Sumatra, W Indonesia 44 A5

Pago Pago W American Samoa 47 D4

Paine, Cerro *Mountain* S Chile 21 B5

Pakistan *Country* S Asia 40 B2

Palau *Country* W Pacific Ocean 45 E4

Palembang Sumatra, W Indonesia 44 B5

Palermo Sicily, Italy 25 D6

Palikir E Micronesia, Pacific Ocean 46 B2

Palma Majorca, Spain 24 C5

Palmer Land *Physical region* Antarctica 53 B2

Palmyra Atoll *Dependent Territory* C Pacific Ocean 47 E2

Palu Celebes, C Indonesia 45 D5

Pampas *Plain* C Argentina 20 C3

Panama City *Country capital* C Panama 15 B3

Panama *Country* Central America 15 C3

Pangkalpinang W Indonesia 44 B5

Papeete W French Polynesia 47 E4

Papua New Guinea *Country* NW Melanesia 50 A1

Paracel Islands *Disputed Dependent Territory* SE Asia 44 C2

Paraguay *Country* C South America 16 C4

Paraguay *River* C South America 16 B6

Paramaribo *Country capital* N Surinam 18 C2

Paraná E Argentina 20 C2

Paraná *River* C South America 20 C2

Parepare Celebes, C Indonesia 45 D5

Paris *Country capital* N France 24 C3

Parkes NSW, SE Australia 49 E4

Parnaíba E Brazil 19 D3

Passo Fundo S Brazil 20 D2

Patagonia *Physical region* Argentina / Chile 21 B5

Patna N India 40 D3

Sendai C Japan 42 F3
Senegal Country W Africa 32 A4
Seoul Country capital NW South Korea 42 D3
Serang Java, C Indonesia 44 B6
Seremban Peninsular Malaysia 44 B4
Serov C Russ. Fed. 27 F1
Sevastopol' S Ukraine 26 C4
Severnaya Zemlya Island group N Russ. Fed. 38 C2
Seville SW Spain 24 B6
Seychelles Island group NE Seychelles 3 B2
Sfax E Tunisia 33 D1
Shackleton Ice Shelf Ice shelf Antarctica 53 B5
Shanghai E China 43 C4
Shangrao S China 43 C5
Shantou S China 43 C5
Shaoguan S China 43 B5
Sharjah Emirate capital NE United Arab Emirates 34 C2
Shebeli River Ethiopia/Somalia 35 D5
Sheffield N England, UK 24 B2
Shenyang NE China 42 C3
Shetland Islands Island group NE Scotland, UK 24 B1
Shijiazhuang E China 42 B3
Shiliguri NE India 40 E3
Shimbiris Mountain N Somalia 35 D5
Shiraz S Iran 34 E2
Shizuoka Honshu, S Japan 43 E4
Shreveport Louisiana, USA 11 E5
Siauliai N Lithuania 25 F2
Siberia Physical region Russ. Fed. 39 D3
Sibiu C Romania 26 A4
Sicily Island Italy, C Mediterranean Sea 25 D6
Sidi Bel Abbès NW Algeria 24 C6
Sidley, Mount Mountain Antarctica 53 A3
Sierra Leone Country W Africa 32 A5
Sierra Madre Mountain range Guatemala/Mexico 3 E2
Simpson Desert Desert Northern Territory/South Australia 49 D3
Singapore Country SE Asia 44 B4
Singkawang C Indonesia 44 C4
Sioux Falls South Dakota, USA 11 E3
Siping NE China 42 D2
Siple, Mount Mountain Siple Island, Antarctica 53 A3
Siracusa Sicily, Italy 25 E6
Sittwe W Burma 40 F3
Sivas C Turkey 26 C5

Skopje Country capital N FYR Macedonia 25 F5
Slovakia Country C Europe 25 E3
Slovenia Country SE Europe 25 E4
Smolensk W Russ. Fed. 26 B2
Snake River River NW USA 10 B3
Sobradinho, Represa de Reservoir E Brazil 19 D4
Sochi SW Russ. Fed. 26 C4
Socotra Island SE Yemen 35 E4
Sofia Country capital Grad Sofiya, W Bulgaria 26 A5
Sohâg C Egypt 34 B2
Sokhumi NW Georgia 27 D4
Solapur W India 41 C4
Solikamsk NW Russ. Fed. 27 F1
Solomon Islands Country W Pacific Ocean 50 D2
Solomon Sea Sea W Pacific Ocean 50 B2
Somalia Country E Africa 35 D5
Sousse NE Tunisia 33 D1
South Africa Country S Africa 30 C6
South America Continent 3 F2
South Australia State S Australia 48 C4
South Carolina State SE USA 12 B5
South China Sea Sea SE Asia 44 C2
South Dakota State N USA 11 D2
South Geomagnetic Pole Pole Antarctica 53 B4
South Georgia Island South Georgia and the South Sandwich Islands, SW Atlantic Ocean 3 B4
South Island Island S NZ 51 D3
South Korea Country E Asia 42 D3
South Orkney Islands Island group Antarctica 53 C2
South Pole Pole Antarctica 53 B3
South Sandwich Islands Island group SE South Georgia and South Sandwich Islands 3 A3
South Shetland Islands Island group Antarctica 53 C2
South West Cape Headland Stewart Island, NZ 51 D3
Southampton S England, UK 24 B3
Southern Ocean Ocean Atlantic Ocean/Indian Ocean/Pacific Ocean 53 C5
Soweto NE South Africa 30 C5
Spain Country SW Europe 24 B5
Spitsbergen Island NW Svalbard 52 B5
Spokane Washington, USA 10 B2

Spratly Islands Disputed Dependent Territory SE Asia 44 C3
Springfield Missouri, USA 11 E4
Sri Lanka Country S Asia 41 D6
St Lucia Country SE West Indies 15 E2
St Pierre and Miquelon French Dependent Territory NE North America 13 E2
St-Nazaire NW France 24 B4
St. Lawrence, Gulf of Gulf NW Atlantic Ocean 13 E2
St.Anthony Newfoundland, Newfoundland and Labrador, SE Canada 13 E1
St.John New Brunswick, SE Canada 13 D2
St.John's E Canada 13 F2
St.Lawrence Seaway River Canada/USA 12 C2
St.Matthias Group Island group NE PNG 50 B1
Stavanger S Norway 24 C1
Stavropol' SW Russ. Fed. 27 D4
Sterlitamak W Russ. Fed. 27 F2
Stettin NW Poland 25 E2
Stockholm Country capital C Sweden 25 E1
Stockton California, USA 10 B4
Stuttgart SW Germany 25 D3
Sucre Country capital S Bolivia 18 B6
Sudan Country N Africa 35 B4
Sudbury Ontario, S Canada 12 B2
Sudd Swamp region S Sudan 35 B5
Suez NE Egypt 34 B2
Sukabumi Java, C Indonesia 44 B6
Sulu Sea Sea SW Philippines 45 D3
Sumatra Island W Indonesia 44 A4
Summer pack ice, limit of Ice feature Antarctica 53 B2
Summer pack ice, limit of Ice feature Arctic Ocean 52 B5
Sumy NE Ukraine 26 C3
Superior, Lake Lake Canada/USA 12 A2
Surabaya Java, C Indonesia 44 C6
Surat W India 41 C4
Surfers Paradise Queensland, E Australia 49 F4
Surinam Country N South America 18 B2
Suva Country capital Viti Levu, W Fiji 50 F3
Svalbard Norwegian Dependent Territory Arctic Ocean 9 E1
Svyataya Anna Trough Undersea feature N Kara Sea 52 C4
Swaziland Country S Africa 31 D5

GLOSSARY OF ABBREVIATIONS
This glossary provides a
comprehensive guide to the
abbreviations used in this index.

CAR Central African Republic

FYR Former Yugoslavian Rebublic

NSW New South Wales

NZ New Zealand

PNG Papua New Guinea

Russ. Fed. Russian Federation

UAE United Arab Emirates

UK United Kingdom

USA United States of America